UNDERSTANDING SCIENCE & NATURE

Physical Forces

TIME-LIFE
ALEXANDRIA, VIRGINIA

CONTENTS

6   Generating Electricity   94

7   The Mysteries of Light   112

8   The Physics of Sound   128

1
Force and Pressure

A number of basic forces exist in the universe and affect the behavior of objects ranging in size from the subatomic to the astronomical. Of these forces, gravity shapes the very fabric of the cosmos and governs the motion of the galaxies, stars, and planets. Gravity also makes its presence felt on the more humble human scale of balloons and boats, airplanes and rockets.

Like all forces, gravity can be measured. Physicists gauge the strength of a force by how it accelerates a body or changes the object's size or shape. Since forces have both magnitude and direction, scientists characterize the forces as vector quantities, which are represented in this book as arrows. When forces act in the same direction, their effect is magnified. When acting in opposite directions, they may cancel each other out; in such a case they are said to be in equilibrium. Force applied against a surface is called pressure and is measured according to its strength across a given area, for instance in pounds per square inch. Gases, liquids, and solids are all subject to the external pressure of the atmosphere, but they also exert internal pressure because of their molecular arrangement. In analyzing phenomena, scientists therefore must frequently consider multiple forces. This book will examine these forces and explain in this chapter how they interact.

In the photograph at right, the gaily colored balloons dotting the sky overcome the force of gravity because they are filled with hot air, which is lighter than the surrounding cold air.

Why Do Things Weigh Less on the Moon?

Objects or people, like the bouncing astronaut shown here, weigh less on the Moon than on Earth because of the Moon's weaker gravitational field. Gravity is a basic force of attraction that is spread throughout the cosmos and acts on all physical objects. The gravitational attraction between any two objects, for example a planet and a person, can be determined by knowing the mass of each item and the distance separating them. Mass, which remains constant, is a measure of the amount of matter an object contains. Weight, on the other hand, is a measure of the force of gravity on an object. The stronger the gravitational field, the greater an object's weight will be and the faster the object will be accelerated; the weaker the field, the less an object's weight will be and the less acceleration it will experience. Since gravity fields vary with the size of the objects they surround, it follows that the weight of an object is not a fixed quantity.

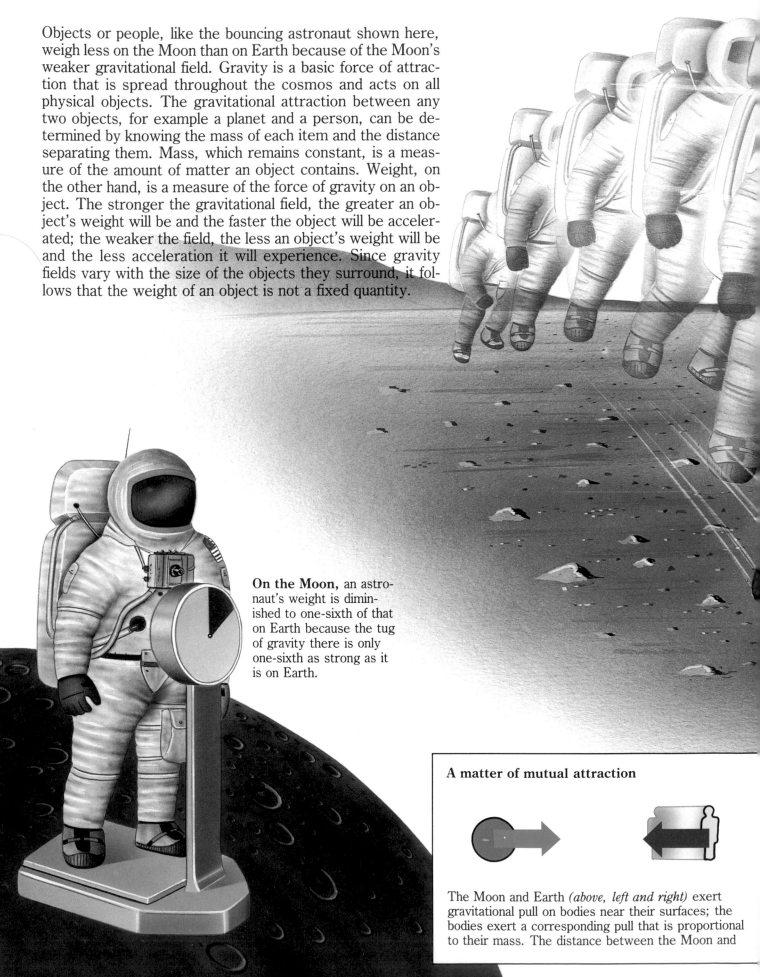

On the Moon, an astronaut's weight is diminished to one-sixth of that on Earth because the tug of gravity there is only one-sixth as strong as it is on Earth.

A matter of mutual attraction

The Moon and Earth *(above, left and right)* exert gravitational pull on bodies near their surfaces; the bodies exert a corresponding pull that is proportional to their mass. The distance between the Moon and

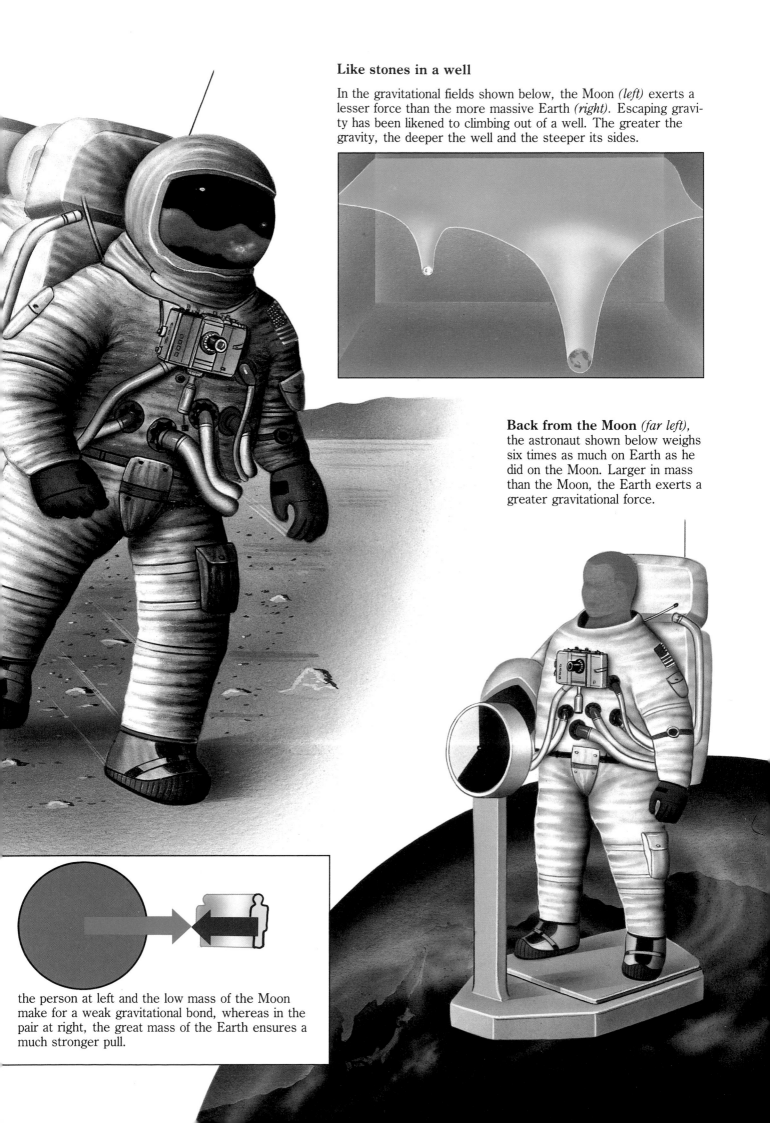

Like stones in a well

In the gravitational fields shown below, the Moon *(left)* exerts a lesser force than the more massive Earth *(right)*. Escaping gravity has been likened to climbing out of a well. The greater the gravity, the deeper the well and the steeper its sides.

Back from the Moon *(far left)*, the astronaut shown below weighs six times as much on Earth as he did on the Moon. Larger in mass than the Moon, the Earth exerts a greater gravitational force.

the person at left and the low mass of the Moon make for a weak gravitational bond, whereas in the pair at right, the great mass of the Earth ensures a much stronger pull.

Why Do Ships Float?

Gravity versus buoyancy

A lightly loaded ship rides high in the water because the force of buoyancy *(blue arrow)* is greater than the tug of gravity *(red arrow)*.

A fully loaded ship sits low in the water, displacing a larger volume of water than a light ship.

Maintaining equilibrium

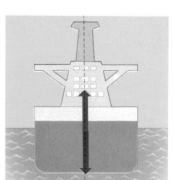

When a ship floats upright, its center of gravity and buoyant force are in line. The ship is in equilibrium.

When a ship tilts, the buoyant force shifts; buoyancy's upward push and gravity's downward pull right the ship.

Ships, boats, rafts, and other objects float because of the buoyant properties of water. Like all liquids, the ocean exerts an upward pressure, which may support solid objects placed on it. In the case of ships, several factors are involved, including the density and shape of the craft and the ways in which it might be buffeted. In general, a ship will float if the volume of water that it displaces weighs more than the ship itself. The upward force of water against the hull will overcome the downward force of gravity, which may be thought of as a single point called the center of gravity. Ships are said to be stable if they can be rocked by such forces as wind or waves and return to an even keel. If a ship is improperly designed or loaded, these disturbances could lead to an unstable ship and it might sink.

Archimedes' principle

The cube below, hanging from a spring scale, weighs less in water *(right)* than in air *(left)*. The cube displaces a volume of water equal in weight to the amount by which its weight has been reduced. The relationship between the volume of a submerged mass and the force that buoys it up was first described by Greek mathematician Archimedes in the third century BC.

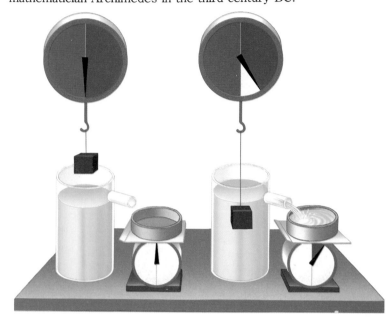

Shifting the center of gravity

Three views show how loads affect a ship's stability. A full hold in the ship at right brings the center of gravity and the center of buoyant force close together, making the ship stable. Tipped by waves, the ship easily rights itself. In the empty ship in the middle, the centers of gravity and of buoyancy have moved far apart, and the ship is unstable. At far right, the weight of flooded ballast tanks restores balance.

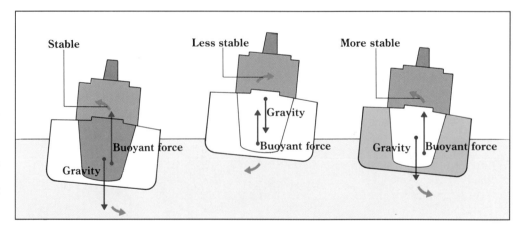

Stable
Less stable
More stable
Gravity
Buoyant force
Gravity
Buoyant force
Gravity
Buoyant force

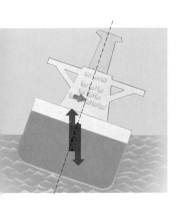

If a tilting ship's center of gravity moves too high and lies too far off the center of buoyancy, the ship will capsize.

Devices that reduce motion

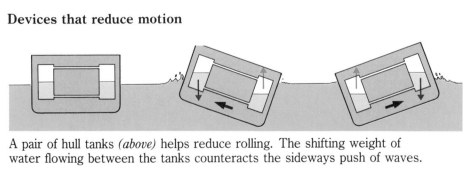

A pair of hull tanks *(above)* helps reduce rolling. The shifting weight of water flowing between the tanks counteracts the sideways push of waves.

A bow tank that alternately takes in and loses water will cause the ship to pitch less in rough seas.

How Do Balloons Stay Up in the Air?

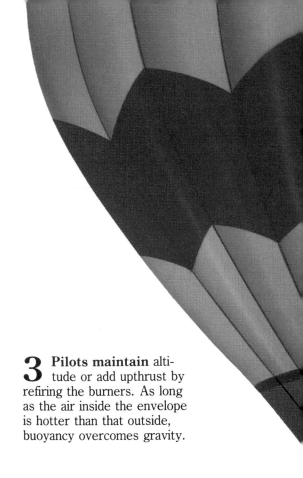

Balloons rise because the gas with which they are filled is lighter than the surrounding air. Many gases, such as hydrogen and helium, are less dense than air. This means that at a given temperature, they have less mass for a certain volume than air. When these lighter-than-air substances are pumped into a balloon, the balloon will rise, as long as the total weight of the envelope, basket, cargo, and lines is less than the weight of the air that the balloon displaces. (Since air is considered a fluid in physics, the same principle governing objects floating in a liquid applies here.) Hot air, which is less dense than cold air, also rises. Although hot air is not as light as some gases, it is safe and easy to produce with propane jets mounted under the mouth of the balloon's envelope, which is usually made of lightweight material such as ripstop nylon. Hot air balloons typically stay aloft for several hours, but without additional heating of the air inside the envelope, they will gradually lose altitude.

3 Pilots maintain altitude or add upthrust by refiring the burners. As long as the air inside the envelope is hotter than that outside, buoyancy overcomes gravity.

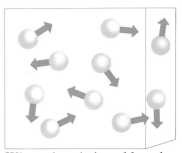

When the air is cold, molecules move slowly and bunch close together.

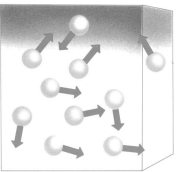

When the air is heated, molecules speed up and separate, filling a larger volume.

2 Hot, lightweight air *(below)* rises inside the envelope and flows down the sides. Cold air is forced out of the mouth. Its weight reduced, the balloon rises.

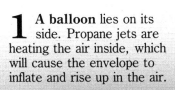

1 A balloon lies on its side. Propane jets are heating the air inside, which will cause the envelope to inflate and rise up in the air.

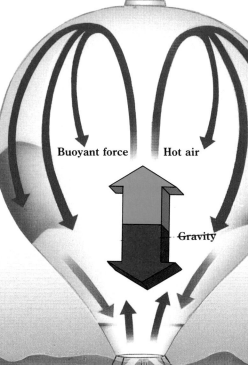

Buoyant force   Hot air

Gravity

Cold air

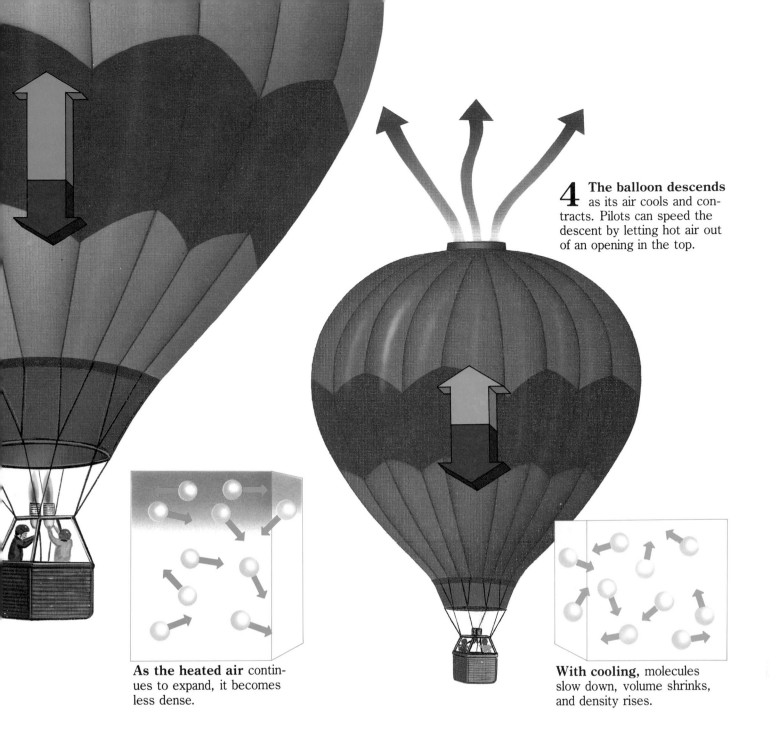

4 **The balloon descends** as its air cools and contracts. Pilots can speed the descent by letting hot air out of an opening in the top.

As the heated air continues to expand, it becomes less dense.

With cooling, molecules slow down, volume shrinks, and density rises.

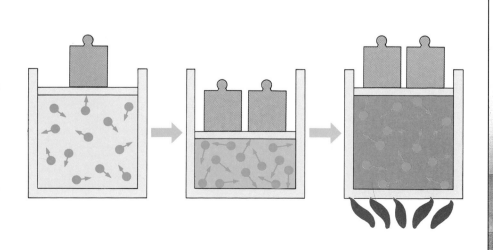

A three-way relationship

The pressure, volume, and temperature of a gas are related. At room temperature *(near right),* the motion of air molecules within a container creates a certain pressure. When the volume is reduced by half *(center),* the internal pressure doubles. When the air is heated *(far right),* its pressure rises and the volume expands in proportion to the temperature increase.

How Can a Boat Sail into the Wind?

A sailboat traveling in the direction of the wind is subject to fairly simple pressure against its sail by the wind, which pushes the craft along. But sailing against the breeze exposes the sail to a more complex set of forces as wind tunnel studies have revealed. When the oncoming air moves past the sail's concave, or curved-in, back side, it is slowed, while around the billowing front side it flows more rapidly. This creates a zone of high pressure behind the sail and a low-pressure zone ahead of it. The difference in pressure on the two sides creates motion, which pushes the boat forward, angled to the wind.

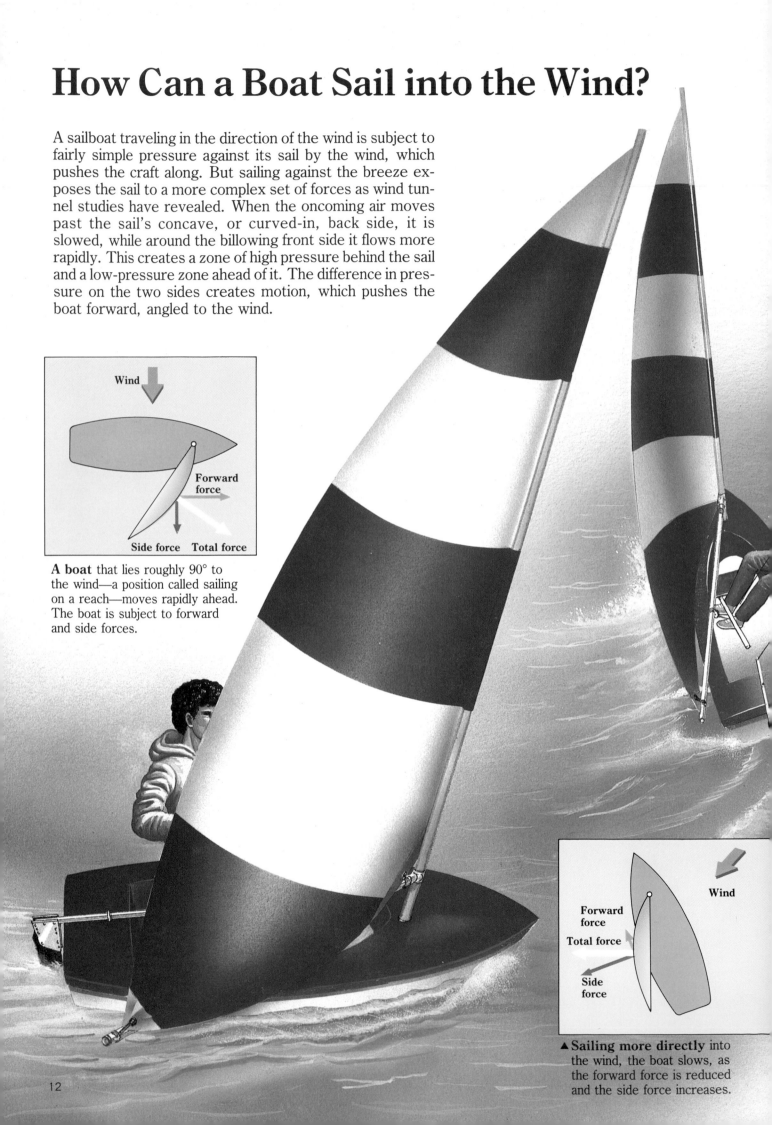

Wind

Forward force

Side force Total force

A boat that lies roughly 90° to the wind—a position called sailing on a reach—moves rapidly ahead. The boat is subject to forward and side forces.

Wind

Forward force

Total force

Side force

▲ **Sailing more directly** into the wind, the boat slows, as the forward force is reduced and the side force increases.

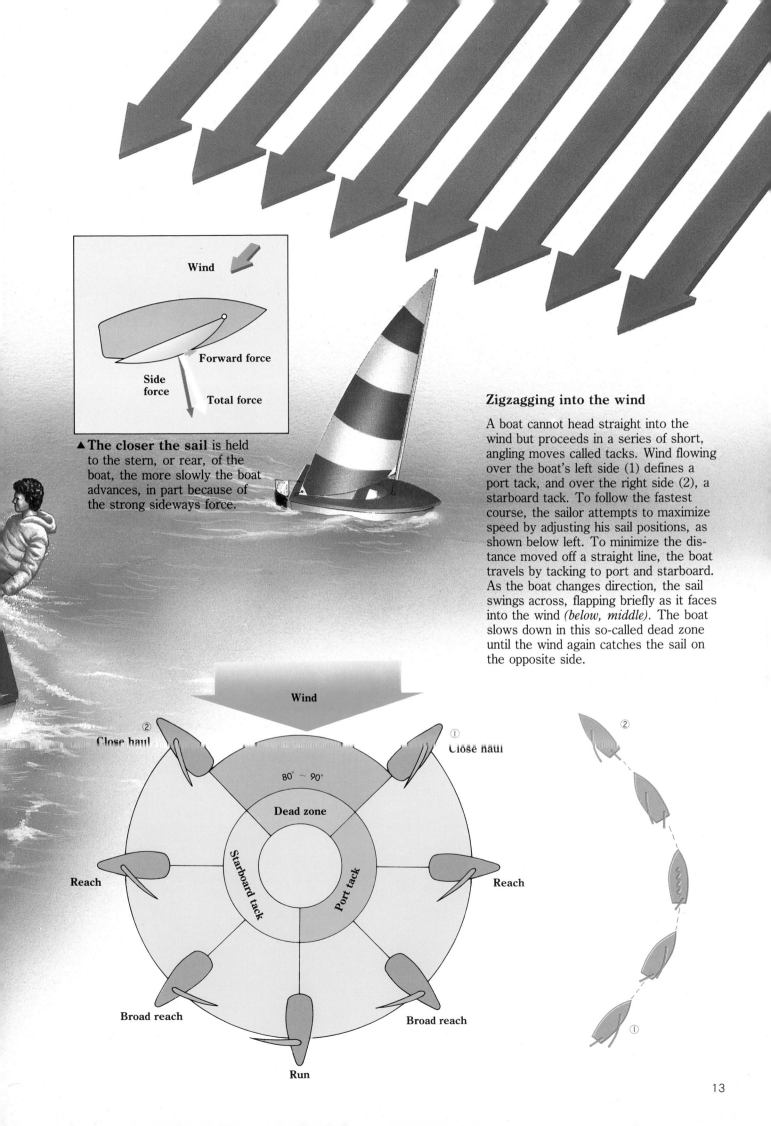

Wind

Forward force

Side force

Total force

▲ **The closer the sail** is held to the stern, or rear, of the boat, the more slowly the boat advances, in part because of the strong sideways force.

Zigzagging into the wind

A boat cannot head straight into the wind but proceeds in a series of short, angling moves called tacks. Wind flowing over the boat's left side (1) defines a port tack, and over the right side (2), a starboard tack. To follow the fastest course, the sailor attempts to maximize speed by adjusting his sail positions, as shown below left. To minimize the distance moved off a straight line, the boat travels by tacking to port and starboard. As the boat changes direction, the sail swings across, flapping briefly as it faces into the wind *(below, middle)*. The boat slows down in this so-called dead zone until the wind again catches the sail on the opposite side.

Wind

② Close haul

① Close haul

80° ~ 90°

Dead zone

Starboard tack

Port tack

Reach

Reach

Broad reach

Broad reach

Run

②

①

How Do Hang Gliders Fly?

The aerodynamic properties of the modern hang glider, which was invented in the 1950s by NASA scientist Francis Rogallo, resemble those of standard aircraft. Launched from a cliff or steep hillside, the moving wing of a glider like the one at right alters the flow of air, which streams more rapidly over the top than over the bottom surface. This creates a low-pressure zone atop the wing and a high-pressure zone underneath, resulting in a force called lift that propels the wing upward. Eddies of air along and behind the wing cause drag, which works to counteract lift. As the front of the wing is angled upward, both lift and drag increase. At too steep a pitch, drag on the wing no longer produces enough lift, and the glider stalls and spins toward the ground out of control.

Forces acting on a glider

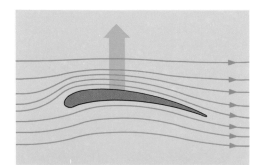

At sufficient speed, a hang glider, a type of airfoil *(purple)*, has enough lift *(green arrow)* to counteract gravity. Favorable winds allow gliders to soar for hours.

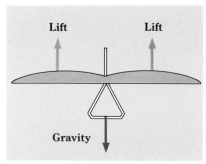

The total lift on the wings must exceed the weight of the glider and the force of gravity for the craft to remain aloft.

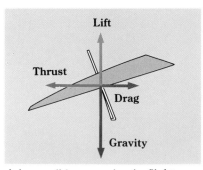

A hang glider remains in flight only if the wing is adjusted to balance the forces that act on it.

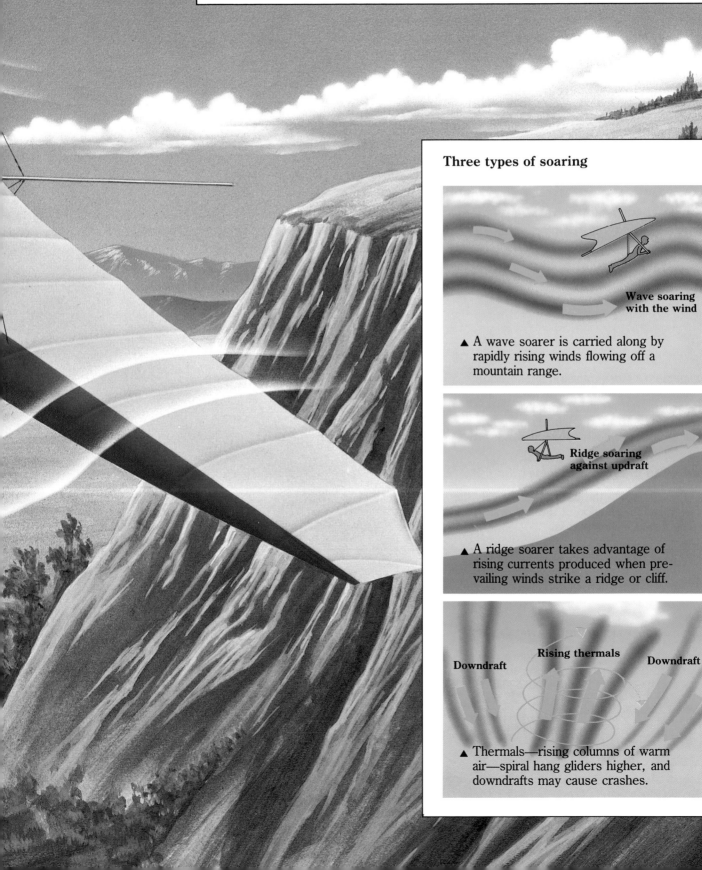

Flying high

A pilot hanging from a harness attached to the wing adjusts his angle of flight by moving the control bar forward. This raises the wing *(far right),* causing the glider to rise and lose speed. Pulling back the bar prompts descent.

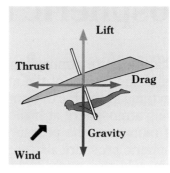

Lift

Thrust

Drag

Gravity

Wind

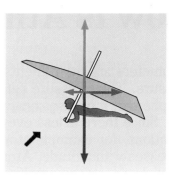

Three types of soaring

Wave soaring with the wind

▲ A wave soarer is carried along by rapidly rising winds flowing off a mountain range.

Ridge soaring against updraft

▲ A ridge soarer takes advantage of rising currents produced when prevailing winds strike a ridge or cliff.

Downdraft　　　Rising thermals　　　Downdraft

▲ Thermals—rising columns of warm air—spiral hang gliders higher, and downdrafts may cause crashes.

How Is a Rocket Launched?

Rockets are lofted into outer space by burning liquid or solid propellants. Ignited in reinforced combustion chambers, these propellants, usually consisting of a fuel and an oxidant, create enormous amounts of pressure and heat, which propel exhaust gases groundward through expansion nozzles. As the exhaust blows down, the rocket blasts off. The phenomenon is described by Newton's third law of motion, which says that for every action there is an equal and opposite reaction. Because liquid fuels are easier to control than solid ones, they are preferred in rockets like the Saturn V shown at left. This three-stage rocket burns thousands of tons of liquid hydrogen and oxygen to boost a capsule into orbit.

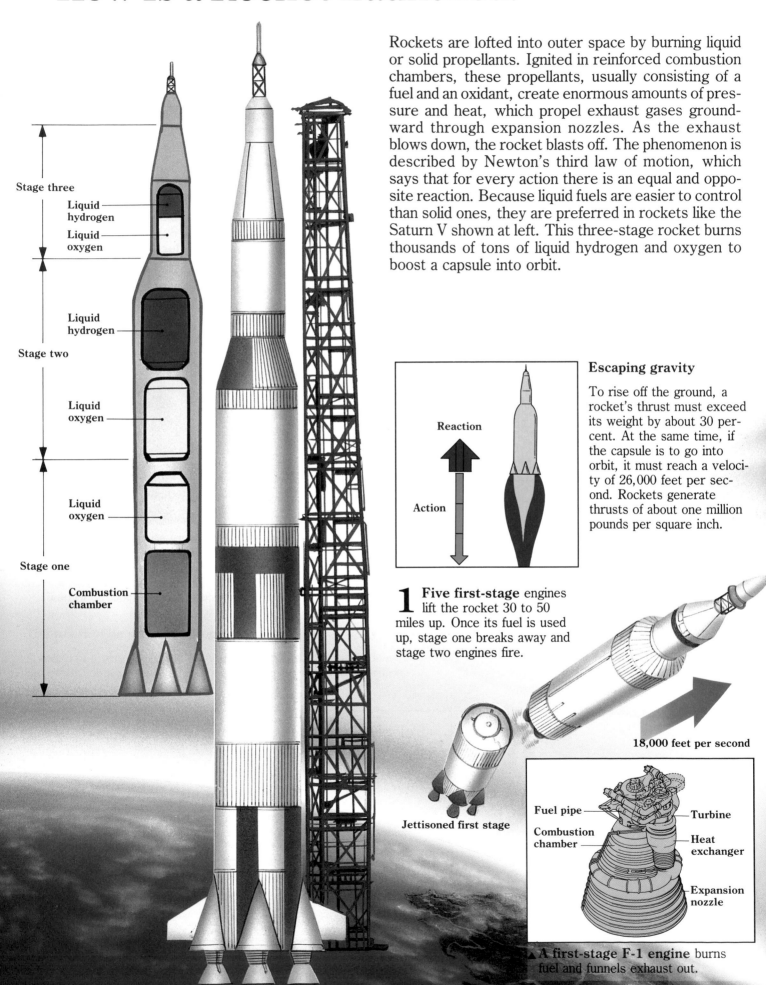

Stage three

Liquid hydrogen

Liquid oxygen

Liquid hydrogen

Stage two

Liquid oxygen

Liquid oxygen

Stage one

Combustion chamber

Escaping gravity

To rise off the ground, a rocket's thrust must exceed its weight by about 30 percent. At the same time, if the capsule is to go into orbit, it must reach a velocity of 26,000 feet per second. Rockets generate thrusts of about one million pounds per square inch.

Reaction

Action

1 **Five first-stage** engines lift the rocket 30 to 50 miles up. Once its fuel is used up, stage one breaks away and stage two engines fire.

18,000 feet per second

Jettisoned first stage

Fuel pipe — Turbine

Combustion chamber — Heat exchanger

Expansion nozzle

▲ **A first-stage F-1 engine** burns fuel and funnels exhaust out.

A trip to the Moon

Once in orbit, the Apollo is shot toward the Moon. Then stage three drops, and the unit composed of command and service modules goes into a 60-mile orbit around the Moon, and the lunar module lands. After ferrying the landing team back, the lunar module will be scuttled.

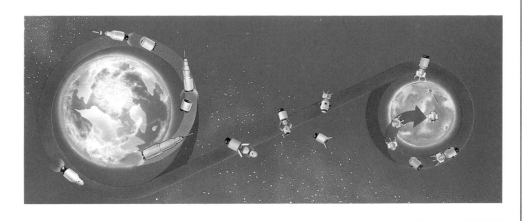

25,600 feet per second

Third-stage burn

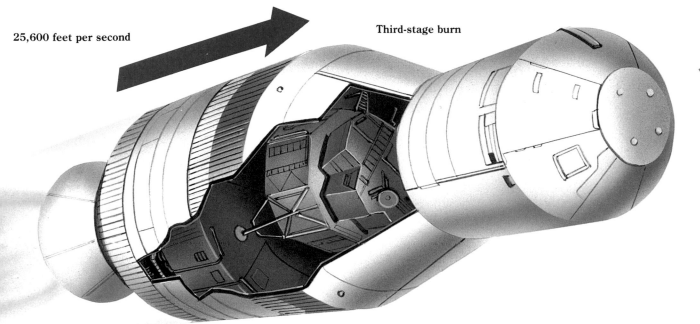

3 **Propelled by** a single third-stage engine, the rocket moves an Apollo spacecraft toward temporary Earth orbit roughly 200 miles up. Shortly, the engine will reignite, boosting speed to about 36,000 feet per second and sending the craft toward the Moon.

2 **About 12 minutes** after lift-off, stage two has carried the rocket more than 100 miles up and falls away empty. The emergency escape rocket also separates.

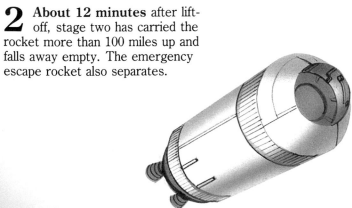

Jettisoned second stage

Emergency escape rocket

19

What Causes Whirlpools to Form?

Natural whirlpools, like the one pictured below, form in oceans, streams, and rivers. They are caused by the interaction of tides or currents, or the presence of objects that deflect the flow of water. But whirlpools may also form when bodies of liquid, like water in sinks or tubs, are emptied down a drain and the water flows down in a spiral. Such a whirlpool, technically called a vortex, is the result of the motion of the individual molecules that make up the liquid. Both gravity and viscosity, or resistance to flow, come into play, as described in the step-by-step drawings at right.

1 When the drain opens, the water molecules immediately above the drain are pulled down by gravity *(below)*. At the same time, resistance to the flow forces the molecules to move in a horizontal direction.

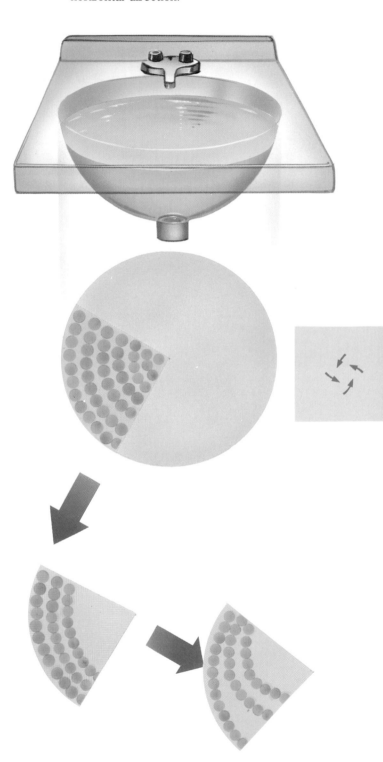

A whirlpool forms in the ocean.

Friction and viscosity

The pie diagram *(right)* traces the path of water molecules as they are set in motion. Gravity pulls down the molecules nearest the drain. Viscosity acts against the pull and the force of friction acts on the surrounding water molecules so that they align and begin to move in tandem.

2 **Once the water** starts to move in a circular path, other water molecules follow. The closer the particles are to the drain, the faster they move. Those farthest from the center travel the slowest.

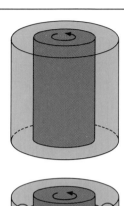

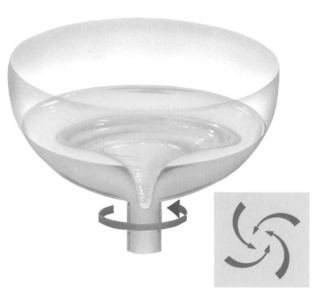

3 **Water spiraling down** the drain forms a depression on the surface of the water, and a column of air builds at the center of the whirlpool.

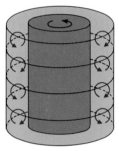

Frictional flow

Water between two cylinders will follow the rotation of the inner cylinder and will spin faster nearer the cylinder than farther away. The different speeds create waves. Eddies form as slow-moving water is taken away by faster flows.

4 **When the water level** in the sink decreases, the air column reaches deeper into the pipe. The vortex builds until all of the water has drained.

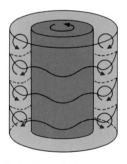

Why Does Water Boil Faster Than Normal at High Altitudes?

30,000 ft.

75° C.
167° F.

20,000 ft.

81° C.
177° F.

90° C.
194° F.

10,000 ft.

100° C.
212° F.

Sea
level

A factor of heat and height

The graph at near right shows the relationship between vapor pressure and temperature. At high temperatures, vapor pressure rises rapidly. Water boils when vapor pressure just exceeds atmospheric pressure. On the other hand, as atmospheric pressure drops, so too will the boiling point. The graph at far right compares altitude to the boiling temperature of water. The higher the altitude, the lower the temperature at which water will boil.

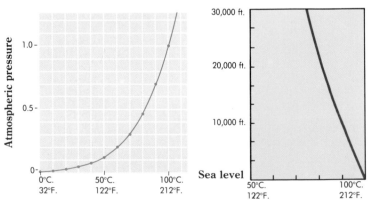

Atmospheric pressure

1.0

0.5

0

0°C.
32°F.

50°C.
122°F.

100°C.
212°F.

30,000 ft.

20,000 ft.

10,000 ft.

Sea level

50°C.
122°F.

100°C.
212°F.

At sea level, water heated to 100° C., or 212° F., begins to boil, which means that bubbles of water vapor form throughout the liquid and rise to the surface. This happens because at that temperature, the vapor pressure of the water slightly exceeds the atmospheric pressure. At higher altitudes, atmospheric pressure is much lower and water boils at lower temperatures. Conversely, if the pressure on a liquid is increased, for instance below sea level or in a pressure cooker, the boiling point is at a higher temperature. The illustration on these pages shows boiling temperatures at various altitudes.

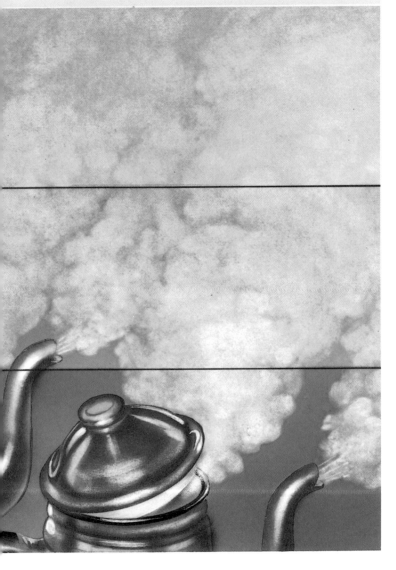

Kinetic energy

Kinetic energy, or the energy of motion of molecules, plays a role when water changes into a gas. When the energy level is high, many molecules evaporate, escaping the bonds that hold them in a liquid state. Under low pressure, below, the molecules acquire enough energy to form gas bubbles for boiling without adding a lot of heat. Closer to sea level, more heat is needed *(red arrow, bottom)* for evaporation to take place.

Lower atmospheric pressure

Higher atmospheric pressure

Speeding cooking time

Pressure cookers, as at right, create a constant, elevated pressure inside. At sea level, the airtight pots boost the temperature at which water boils to 121° C., or 250° F. Higher temperature means that foods cook faster, saving time.

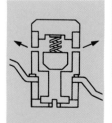
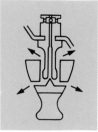

Cutaway views show pressure cooker mechanisms that prevent explosive pressures from building. The emergency safety valve *(left)*, the regulator *(center)*, and the packing at the rim *(right)* all help to control pressure by allowing steam to escape.

2
Gravity and Motion

The motion of everything in the universe—from atoms and molecules to stars and galaxies—is governed by a few fundamental laws. The best formulation of these laws comes from English physicist Sir Isaac Newton, who in 1687 shook the scientific world with his book *The Mathematical Principles of Natural Philosophy*. In addition to describing a theory of universal gravitation, this book listed the three laws of motion.

Newton's first law of motion states that moving objects continue to move in a straight line and objects at rest remain at rest, unless acted on by an outside force. Called inertia *(pages 28-29),* this principle plays a role in moving bodies from roller coasters to satellites. The second law describes how a force acting on an object causes acceleration. The amount of acceleration is determined by both the size of the force and the mass of the object. The third law states that for every action there is an equal and opposite reaction. In the case of rockets, it is the combustion of tons of fuel (the action) that provides the thrust (the reaction) necessary for liftoff.

Although Newton's laws are now so familiar they are taught in most schools, when first published they were nothing short of astounding. Such seemingly unrelated phenomena as the falling of an apple and the orbiting of planets around the Sun were from then on described under one theory.

Governed by the laws of motion, rotating objects display unusual patterns like the break of a curve ball and the wobble of a spinning top *(right).*

How Can Skiers Move So Quickly?

Skiers can race downhill—often at more than 100 miles per hour—because they are able to overcome friction, the force that prevents sliding between two objects. When a skier first steps onto a slope, friction causes the skis to stick to the snow. But the skier's weight exerts a force perpendicular to the slope that melts a thin layer of snow under the skis, creating a film of water. This film acts as a lubricant, greatly reducing the braking force of friction and allowing the force of gravity to pull the skier down the slope. As the skier moves forward, heat generated by the skis sliding against the snow continuously melts new snow underneath the skis, maintaining the watery film. A skier can gain even more speed by coating the bottoms of the skis with wax, which repels water and further reduces friction.

For the same reason, ice skaters glide over a thin film of water, rather than on the ice itself. The great pressure that is exerted by the skates' narrow blades causes the ice to melt, nearly eliminating friction.

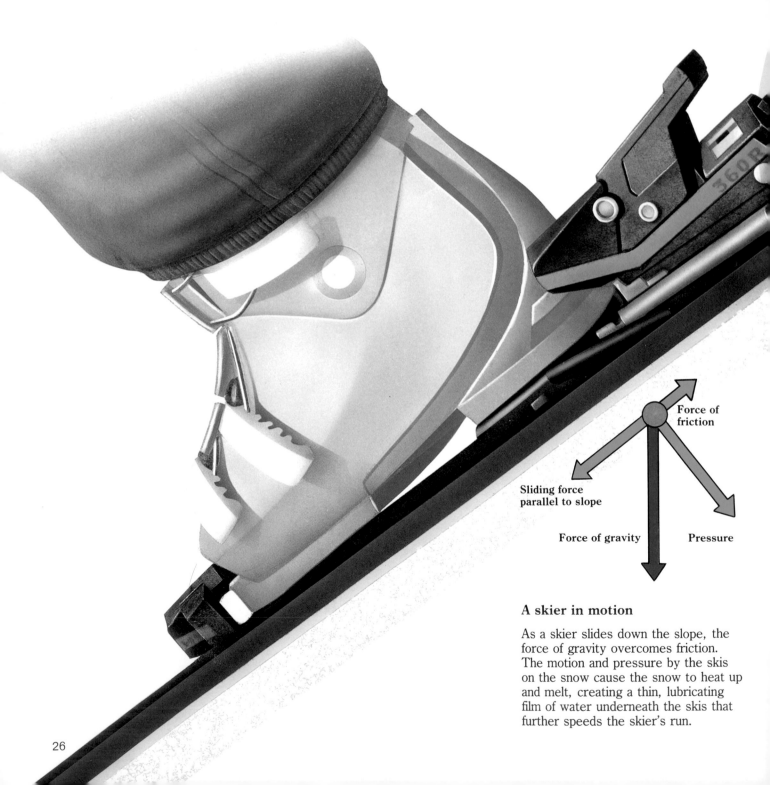

Force of friction

Sliding force parallel to slope

Force of gravity

Pressure

A skier in motion

As a skier slides down the slope, the force of gravity overcomes friction. The motion and pressure by the skis on the snow cause the snow to heat up and melt, creating a thin, lubricating film of water underneath the skis that further speeds the skier's run.

A skier starting out

At first, the force of friction between the skis and the snow presents a barrier to a skier's downward motion. But once the skier's weight exerts pressure on the snow, the snow begins to melt and the skier glides down.

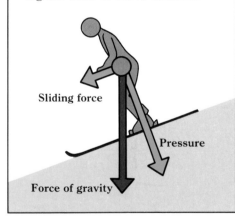

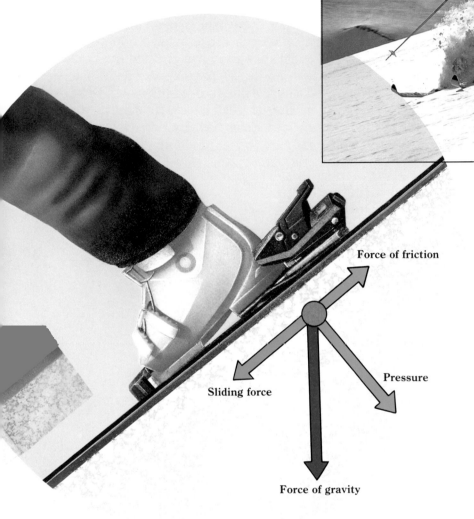

Force of friction

Sliding force

Pressure

Force of gravity

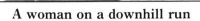

A woman on a downhill run

The forces acting on a skier

For a skier on a slope, the force of gravity has two components: One is perpendicular to the slope and pushes down on the snow; one is parallel to the slope, causing the skier to move downhill.

Sliding force

Pressure

Force of gravity

Skating on ice

Like skiers, ice skaters move on a layer of water between the ice and the skates. The enormous pressure of the blades on the ice lowers the freezing point of the ice enough so that the surface of the ice begins to melt. The more the pressure increases, the more the ice will melt and the faster the skater will glide along.

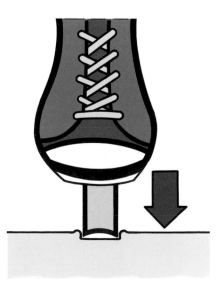

What Is Inertia?

Objects do not move on their own unless a force sets them in motion or changes their direction. The resistance to change is called inertia, which means simply that bodies at rest remain at rest, and moving bodies remain in motion unless acted on by outside forces. When an electric fan is turned off, for example, the rapidly spinning blades continue to turn for a while before slowing down and stopping. Were it not for the friction between the blades and the motor, and air resistance, the blades would spin indefinitely even though the fan was off. But once the blades have stopped spinning, they will not start again on their own. A force, in this case an electric motor,

is necessary to start the fan. The tendency of all objects to retain their state of motion—whether stationary or moving—explains why passengers standing on a train fall backward or forward when the train starts or stops *(below)*.

Ever since the Greek philosopher Aristotle investigated inertia more than 2,000 years ago, many great thinkers have puzzled over the concept. In 1635, Italian physicist Galileo Galilei performed a series of experiments using balls rolling down inclines that led him to the first modern description of inertia. Building on Galileo's work, Sir Isaac Newton summed up his findings on inertia as the first of his three laws of motion.

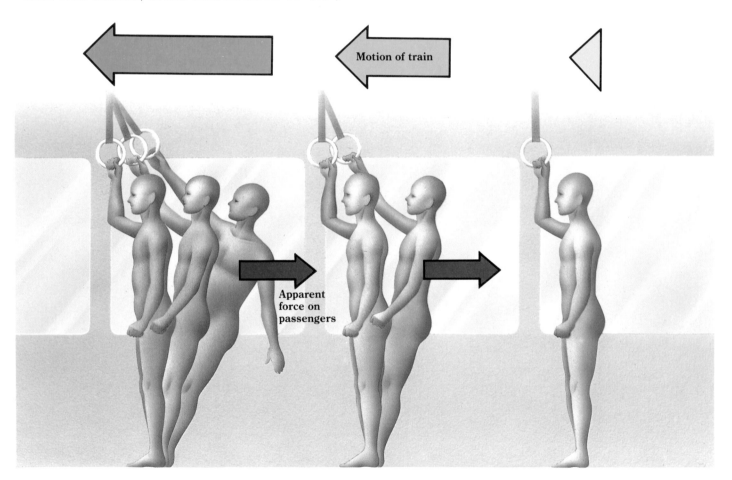

Motion of train

Apparent force on passengers

Bodies at rest

As shown in the illustration above, passengers are caught unawares when the train starts to move, and they begin to fall backward. The diagram at right shows how the hand strap carries, or transfers, the force that is needed to shift the riders forward, while gravity holds them in place. The passengers react to the acceleration as if an invisible force is pulling them backward.

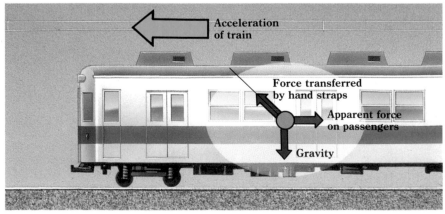

Acceleration of train

Force transferred by hand straps

Apparent force on passengers

Gravity

Galileo's experiment

Through his observations of balls rolled along inclined planes, Galileo was able to correctly describe inertia. If there were no friction to slow things down, a ball rolled down an incline would continue to roll up a second incline *(top)* until the force of gravity overcame its kinetic energy, or energy of motion. In the middle example, the ball travels farther along the second incline than in the top example, since the second incline is not as steep. Galileo reasoned that as the angle of the second incline decreased, the ball would roll farther before giving in to gravity. If the second plane were horizontal, as in the bottom example, gravity would not affect motion, and the ball would roll forever.

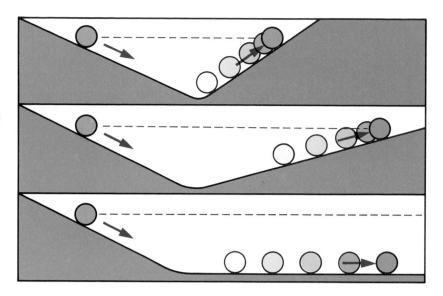

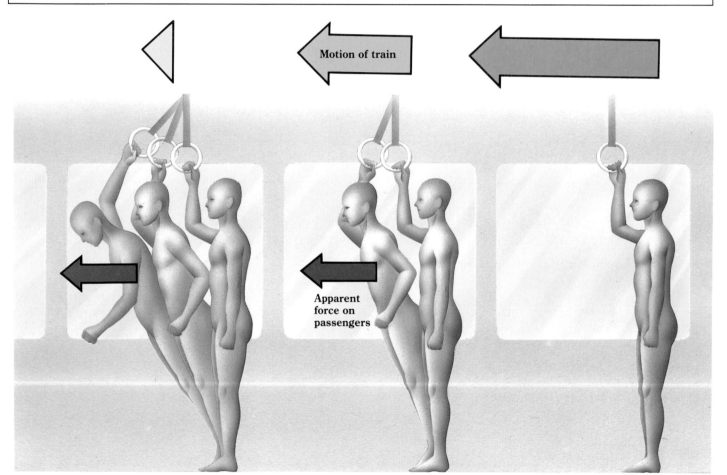

Motion of train

Apparent force on passengers

Bodies in motion

As a moving train slows down, its brakes exert a force opposite to the direction of motion *(blue arrow)* to stop it. Since there is no similar braking force for passengers standing inside the train, they keep moving and fall forward. The force transferred through the hand strap and the force of gravity transmit that stopping force to the passengers. The abrupt change in motion makes the riders feel as though a force pushed them forward.

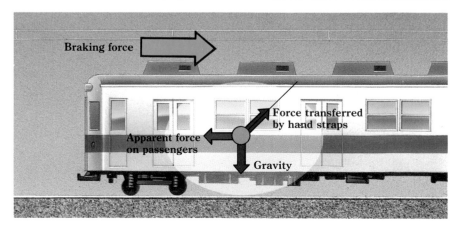

Braking force

Force transferred by hand straps

Apparent force on passengers

Gravity

Why Don't People Fall Out of an Upside-Down Roller Coaster?

When a hurtling roller coaster enters a loop-the-loop, several forces besides the safety precautions of special wheels and lap bars keep passengers and cars from plunging to the ground. Inertia *(pages 28-29)* propels the cars in a straight line, while the rails of the circular track press against them so that the cars seem to be held against the track. The curve of the track and the effects of gravity on the cars combine to create a centripetal, or "center-seeking," force. Although riders feel as though some separate force is pressing them outward against their seats, they are merely experiencing the centripetal force caused by the curved rails and the gravity working against and balancing the inertia of the moving cars. The combination of inertia and centripetal force is often called centrifugal, or "center-fleeing," force. Centrifugal force does not actually exist, but people sometimes use the term as a short-cut explanation.

Building momentum

To make it through a loop, a car must have a lot of momentum—a product of its mass and speed. If the momentum is too small, the so-called centrifugal force will not exceed the force of gravity and the car will fall off. But if the launching hill is high and steep enough, the cars will have enough momentum to roll through and out of the loop.

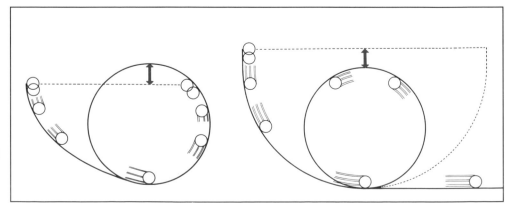

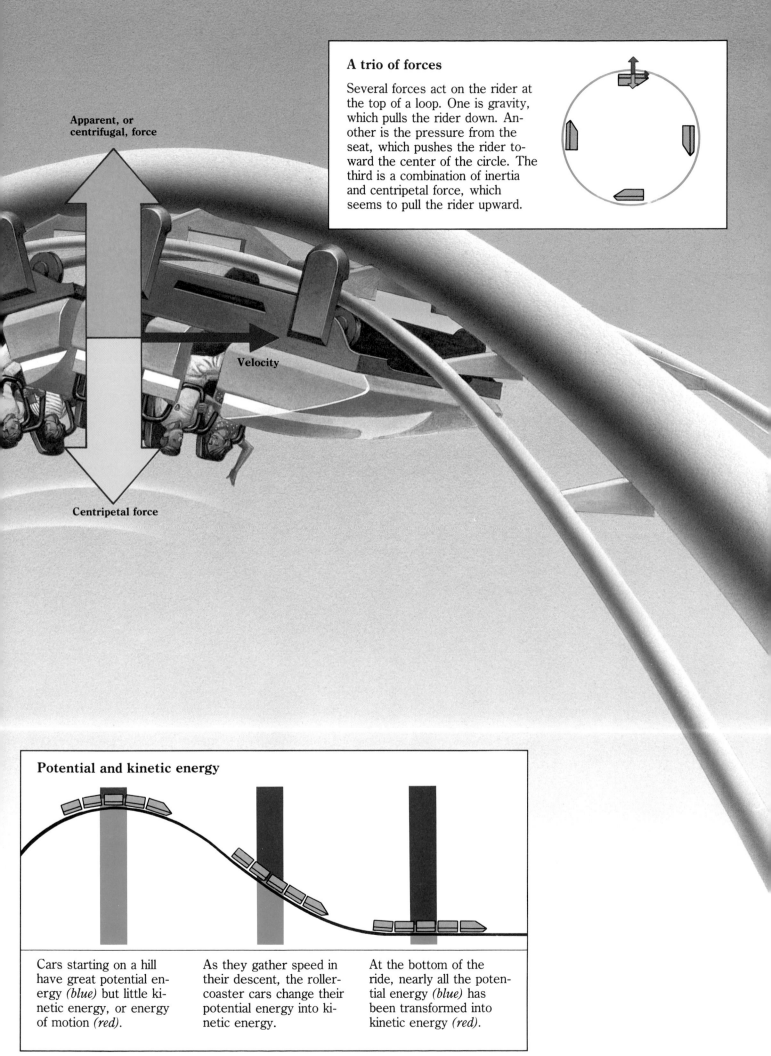

Apparent, or centrifugal, force

Velocity

Centripetal force

A trio of forces

Several forces act on the rider at the top of a loop. One is gravity, which pulls the rider down. Another is the pressure from the seat, which pushes the rider toward the center of the circle. The third is a combination of inertia and centripetal force, which seems to pull the rider upward.

Potential and kinetic energy

Cars starting on a hill have great potential energy *(blue)* but little kinetic energy, or energy of motion *(red)*.

As they gather speed in their descent, the roller-coaster cars change their potential energy into kinetic energy.

At the bottom of the ride, nearly all the potential energy *(blue)* has been transformed into kinetic energy *(red)*.

How Can a Spinning Top Stay Upright?

Although a stationary top cannot be balanced on its end, a spinning top can stay upright for minutes. Spinning tops, as well as all other rotating bodies, possess a property called angular momentum—the product of the top's distribution of mass and its rate of spin—that produces a rotating force. Called a torque, this force causes the top's spin axis to rotate rather than fall over and produces the familiar wobble, technically known as precession. As friction between the ground and the top makes the top lose some of its angular momentum, the top begins to slow down and fall.

While spinning tops are fun to play with, their properties serve far more useful functions elsewhere. Their most important application lies in the gyroscope, which is little more than a top mounted on a pivoting cradle. Extremely sensitive to changes in direction, which affect its precession, the gyroscope is essential to the navigational systems of planes and boats, and has made possible the remote-controlled guidance of spacecraft.

Z

Torque

Precession

Center of mass
G

Force perpendicular to ground

Point of contact with the ground

O

Pull of gravity

Precession

Constantly buffeted by gravity, a spinning top uses its angular velocity and gravity's downward pull to produce a sideways torque. This torque causes the top's spin axis to rotate, or precess, in a circle around its vertical axis (O/Z). The angle at which the top leans while tracing out the circle increases as the top loses angular momentum.

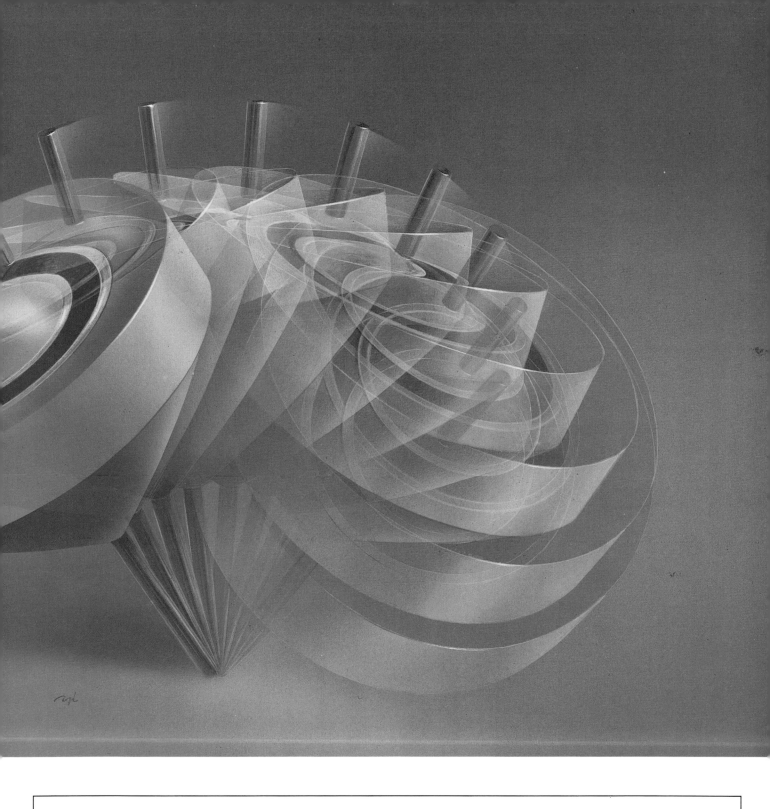

The upside-down top

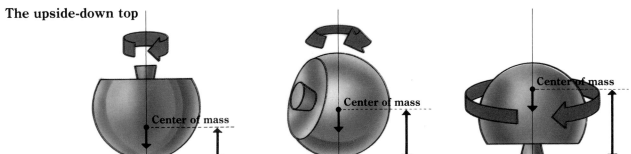

An upside-down top will turn over and begin spinning on its handle *(above, right).* The secret to this trick lies in its center of gravity. Spinning tops are most stable when their centers of gravity lie high off the ground. When this kind of top begins to spin *(above, left),* its gravitational center is near the ground. To raise its cen-ter of gravity, the top spins on its side and converts some of its kinetic energy into potential energy by turning upside down, gaining far more stability.

Why Does a Baseball Curve?

People sometimes say that baseballs don't really curve, that it's just an optical illusion. Baseball players and scientists know better. A major league pitcher can make a ball curve, drop, or hop as it flies toward home plate. The trajectory of a pitch is determined by the speed and direction of the spin imparted to the ball as it leaves the pitcher's hand. According to the laws of physics, any object, such as a baseball moving through air, is subject to a variety of physical forces, which combine to affect the course of the object's motion.

A baseball is sewn together with 216 stitches of red thread. Once the ball is in flight, the stitches carry a layer of air with them as the ball rotates. The air travels slightly faster on the side of the ball in the direction of the spin. The more rapidly air moves, the less pressure it exerts. Thus, air pressure is lower on the side of the ball in the direction of the spin and greater on the opposite side. Just as weather systems move from areas of high to low pressure, the baseball curves in the direction of its spin toward the low-pressure area. A major league curve ball rotates about 18 times during its half-second flight to the plate and may curve by as much as 17½ inches.

Rotation and the Magnus effect

As a ball moves, it encounters drag, or resistance, from the air. Drag is less on the side of the ball in the direction of its spin. This imbalance creates a force at a right angle to the direction of the ball's flight. Known as the Magnus effect, the force is proportional to spin rate, velocity, and drag.

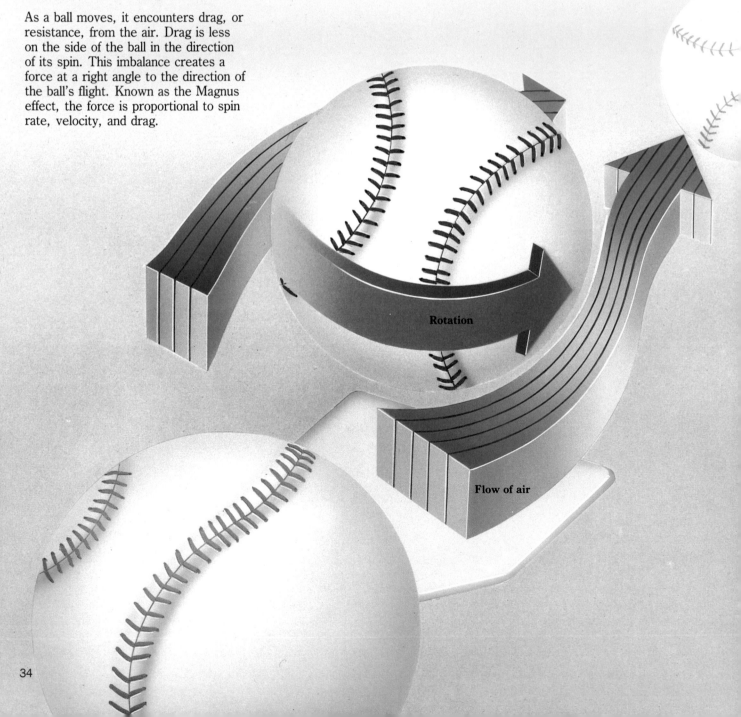

Rotation

Flow of air

The curve ball

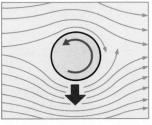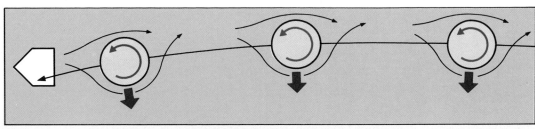

A pitcher throws a curve ball by twisting his wrist to make the ball spin. A right-hander's curve spins downward and counterclockwise (as seen from above), causing the ball to drop and resulting in a movement, or break, toward the right side of home plate. As the flow of air is faster on the side of the ball in the direction of the spin, the ball breaks in that direction.

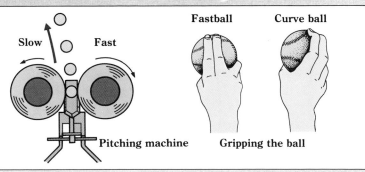

The screwball

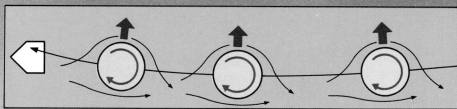

A screwball is thrown by twisting the wrist toward the body, instead of away from the body as in a curve ball. This twist gives the ball the opposite spin from a curve and causes it to break in the reverse direction. A right-hander's screwball breaks toward a right-handed batter.

The fastball

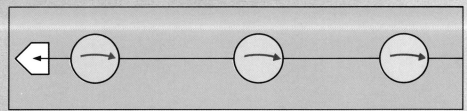

A good fastball is not simply a straight pitch, but it also has its own special movement. At the point of release, the pitcher pulls downward on the seams, causing the ball to rotate backward toward the pitcher. This results in a Magnus effect directed upward and causes the ball to hop. A 90-mile-per-hour fastball may hop as much as 4 inches.

Putting spin on the ball

The difference between a fastball, curve ball, and screwball is in the speed and direction of the ball's spin. The Magnus effect causes a ball to break in the direction in which it is spinning. A pitching machine creates differing spins by varying the speeds of the two ejector wheels. A pitcher does it by changing his grip on the ball.

How Do Satellites Stay in Orbit?

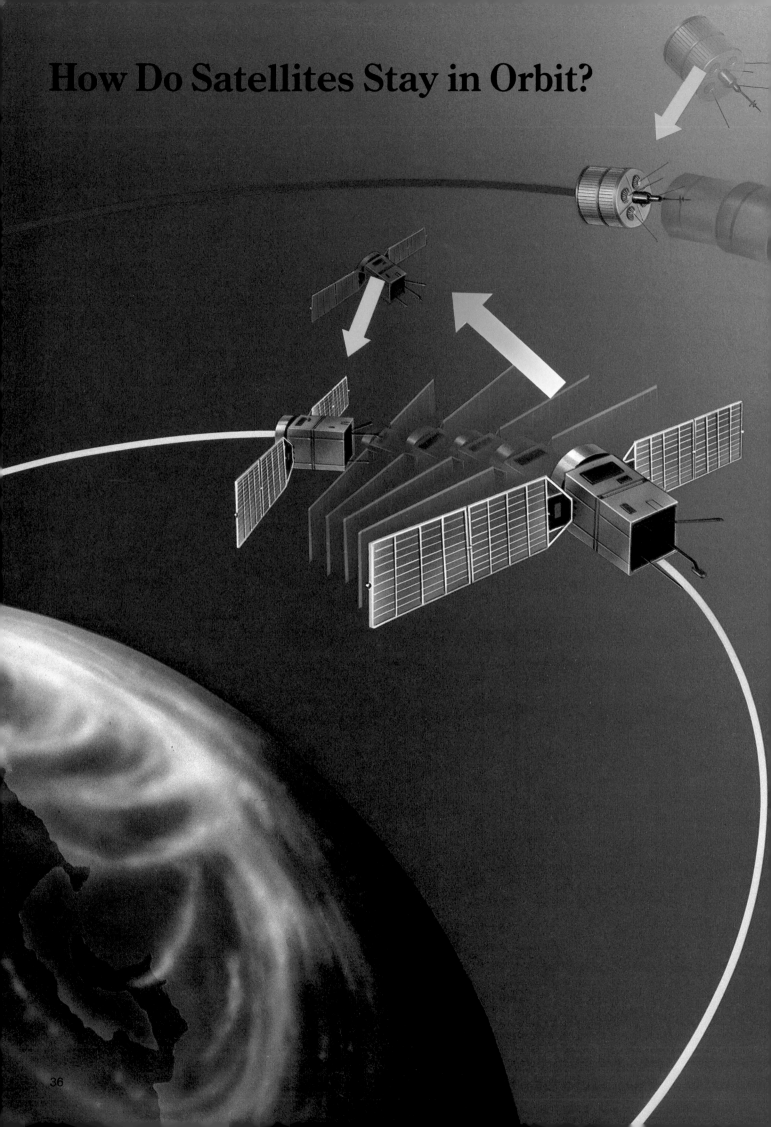

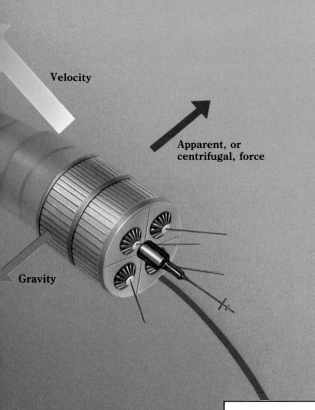

Velocity

Apparent, or centrifugal, force

Gravity

A satellite's orbit represents a delicate balance between inertia and gravity. The force of gravity is continuously pulling the satellite toward Earth, while the satellite's inertia keeps it moving in a straight line. If it were not for gravity, the satellite's inertia would send it straight out of Earth's orbit and into space. But at every point in the orbit, gravity reins in the satellite.

To reach a balance between inertia and gravity, the satellite must be moving at a precise speed. If it moves too fast, inertia overcomes gravity and the satellite leaves orbit. (The calculation of the speed that would propel a satellite out of Earth's orbit, that is, the escape velocity, plays an important role in the launching of space probes.) If the satellite moves too slowly, gravity wins its battle with inertia and the satellite plummets to Earth. That is just what happened in 1979, when the American space station Skylab began slowing down as a result of drag from the outer fringes of Earth's atmosphere. Gravity's unyielding grip then brought the spacecraft crashing down to Earth.

Speed and distance

Since the pull of gravity lessens with distance, the velocity needed to keep a satellite in orbit varies with altitude. Engineers can calculate how fast and how high a satellite must orbit. For example, a geostationary satellite—one that always remains over the same point on Earth—must circle the planet once every 24 hours, matching Earth's rotation, at an altitude of 22,300 miles.

Gravity and inertia

The balancing act a satellite performs with gravity and inertia can be mimicked by swinging a weight tied to a string. The weight's inertia pulls it constantly outward, while the tension in the string—playing the role of gravity—keeps the weight in a circular orbit. If the string were cut, the weight would fly off in a straight path perpendicular to the radius of its orbit.

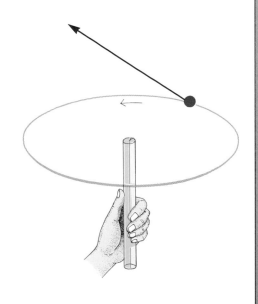

How Can Surfers Ride Waves?

The apparent effortlessness with which experienced surfers race over waves belies the complexity of the forces that make surfing possible. Waves vary in shape tremendously between their point of origin and the shore, and it is only close to the beach where rising swells approach their first break that surfers can ride them.

Generated by ocean currents, wind, and the moon's tidal pull, waves begin their lives in the deep ocean, far from any beach. As they move toward shore, they slow down and bunch up, becoming taller and narrower *(below, right)*. Surfers take advantage of this motion by catching a wave as it begins to break. Standing slightly to the rear of center on their boards to balance their weight and keeping the noses of the boards clear of the water, surfers maneuver their boards sideways across the wave. The surfboard is thrust forward by a combination of the force of gravity, buoyancy, and the wave's forward motion. In essence, the board slides down the wave as it moves ashore.

Catching a wave

When a surfer begins a ride, the wave is shallow and moves quickly to shore. But as the wave approaches the beach, it slows down and becomes steeper, challenging the surfer to maintain his balance as the wave crests.

Deep ocean waves

Waves far from shore are too shallow and too fast for surfing. As a wave approaches, an object such as the block of wood shown below is pushed up and slightly forward. But as the wave passes, the block slides back to the starting point.

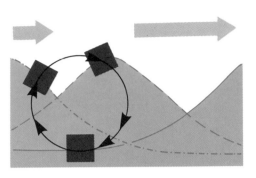

A surfer slides down a breaking wave.

History of a wave

Wave on the open sea

When waves originate far out at sea, they are broad and symmetrically shaped, and move very quickly.

Wave nearing the beach

As waves approach the shallower bottom near the beach, they slow down and bunch up, toppling over themselves.

3
Simple Machines

Most modern machines, no matter how sophisticated, consist of combinations of a few basic moving parts. Called simple machines by physicists, these parts—the lever, the inclined plane, and the wheel—have served mankind since the dawn of civilization. With the exception of electronic devices, today's highly complex mechanized marvels are direct descendants of tools used thousands of years ago to cut down trees, build shelters, and erect the great pyramids.

Physicists define the five types of simple machines as the lever, the wheel and axle, the pulley, the inclined plane, and the screw. Each works in one of three ways. It can take the force exerted by a person and redirect it, for example by allowing the person to pull on an object, rather than push. It can turn a small effort or force into a larger force, a concept known as mechanical advantage. Or it can magnify the distance that a force acts on. While these machines do not reduce the amount of work needed to perform a task, they do reduce the effort required from the user. With the proper simple machines, used either alone or in combination, even the most formidable of tasks can be made easier.

From construction cranes to can openers to most of the tools shown at right, mechanical devices rely on just a few simple principles.

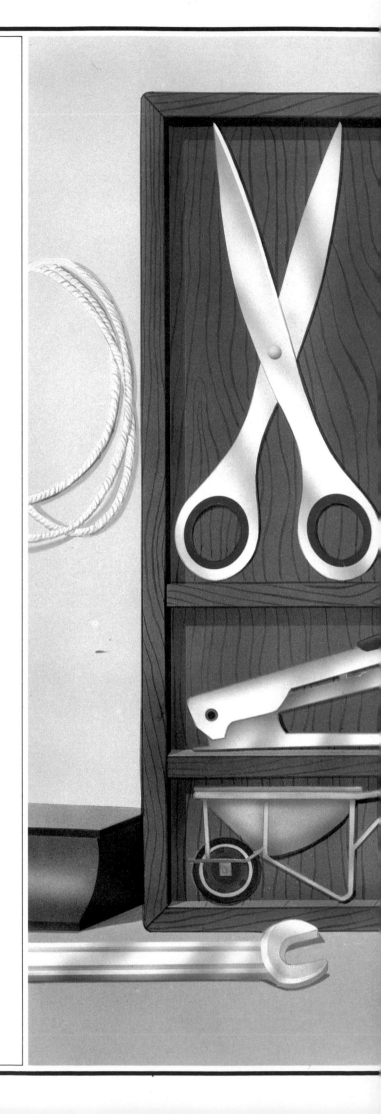

What Are Levers?

A lever is a narrow beam that rotates around a single point, called the fulcrum. By placing an object to be moved, called a load, at one point on the beam and applying an effort at another point, a person can move the object far more easily than by picking it up and moving it by hand.

Levers work by a simple formula: The effort multiplied by its distance from the fulcrum equals the weight multiplied by its distance from the fulcrum. The longer the lever arm, the greater the force amplification, and the easier it becomes to move the load. The price for this advantage is that the longer the lever arm is, the shorter the distance the load will move.

As illustrated below, there are three classes of levers, which differ by the relative positions of the applied force, the load, and the fulcrum.

Second-class levers

In a second-class lever, the fulcrum lies at one end, an effort is applied at the other end, and the load (W) lies in between, as shown in the pink diagram at right. The wheelbarrow, bottle opener, stapler, and paper punch are members of this class in which any effort is magnified.

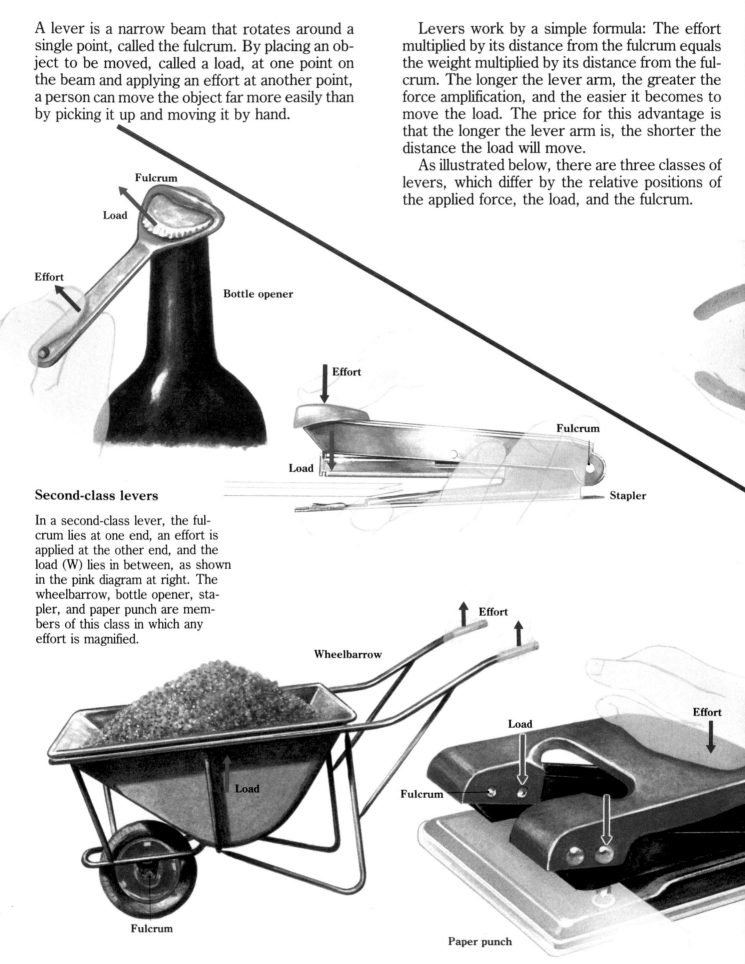

Fulcrum

Load

Effort

Bottle opener

Effort

Load

Fulcrum

Stapler

Effort

Wheelbarrow

Load

Fulcrum

Load

Fulcrum

Effort

Paper punch

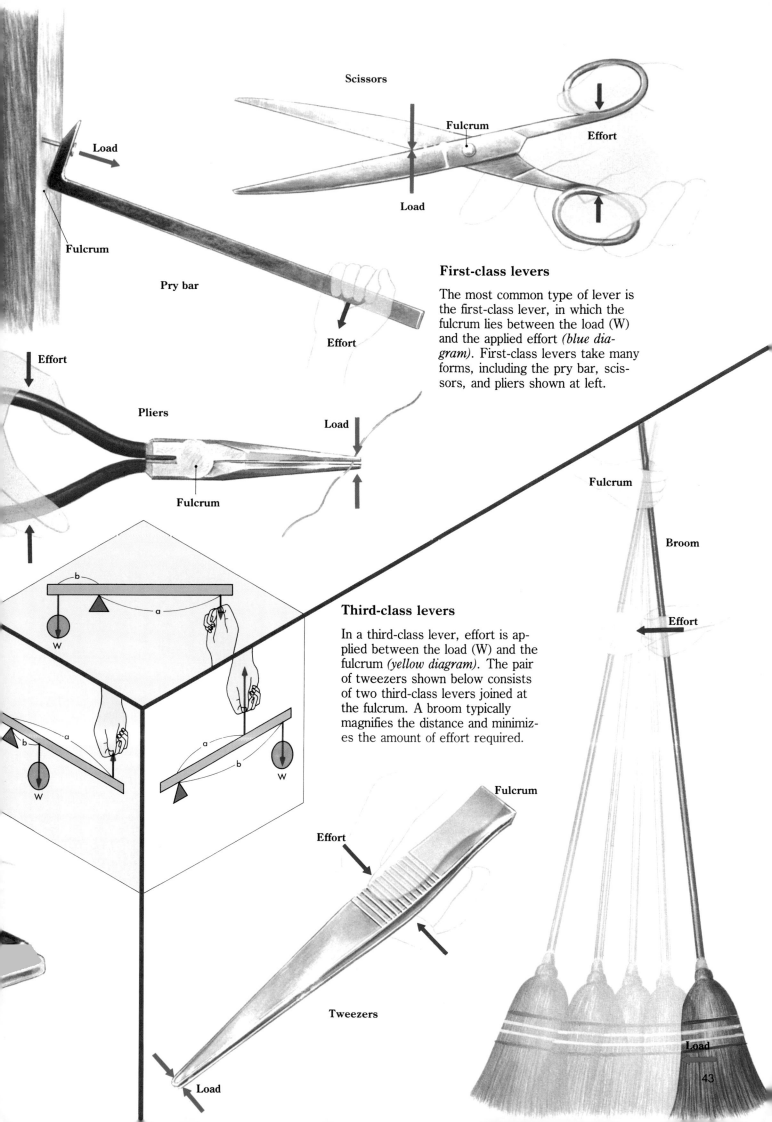

Scissors

Fulcrum

Effort

Load

Load

Fulcrum

Pry bar

Effort

Effort

Pliers

Load

Fulcrum

First-class levers

The most common type of lever is the first-class lever, in which the fulcrum lies between the load (W) and the applied effort *(blue diagram)*. First-class levers take many forms, including the pry bar, scissors, and pliers shown at left.

Fulcrum

Broom

Effort

Third-class levers

In a third-class lever, effort is applied between the load (W) and the fulcrum *(yellow diagram)*. The pair of tweezers shown below consists of two third-class levers joined at the fulcrum. A broom typically magnifies the distance and minimizes the amount of effort required.

Fulcrum

Effort

Tweezers

Load

Load

43

How Do Inclined Planes Work?

Like levers, inclined planes reduce the effort needed to raise an object. For example, a block weighing 100 pounds would be difficult to lift, but it can easily be raised by sliding it up a ramp. Placing the block on a tilted surface divides its weight into two components, one parallel and one perpendicular to the surface. To move the block up the ramp, a person needs only to overcome the parallel component, the magnitude of which increases with the ramp's tilt.

Inclined planes take many forms. The screw, for example, consists of an inclined plane, which is the screw's thread, wrapped around a cylinder. When the screw is turned, the threads dig deeper into an object and hold tight by virtue of the great friction that exists between the object and the threads. The vise converts lever action and the screw's rotary motion into straight-line pressure, as does the jackscrew, which lifts objects by the same principle.

The vise

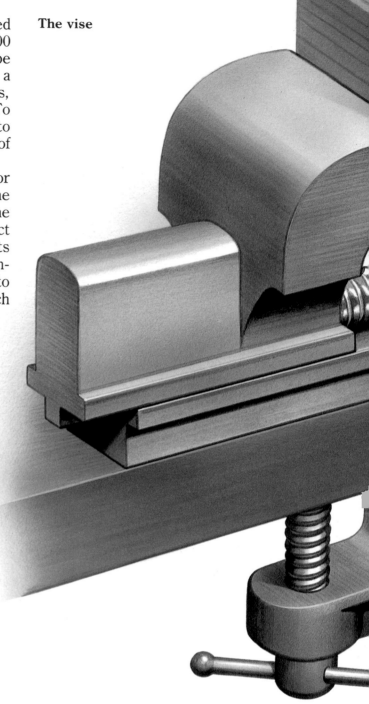

Forces on an inclined plane

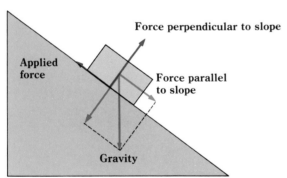

For an object on an incline, gravity is exerted parallel and perpendicular to the plane. Pushing the object up the incline requires a force equal to that of the parallel component of gravity.

Planes and screws

It is easy to see the screw's relation to the inclined plane by wrapping a paper cutout around a cylinder. The resulting spiral is identical to the pattern of threads on a screw.

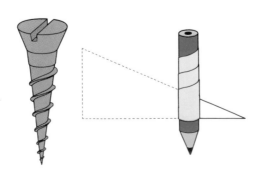

Force and work. Although an inclined plane can make a task easier, it does not reduce the amount of work required for performing the task. Lifting a block of 100 pounds (W) 30 feet straight up *(far right)* requires a force equal to 100 x 30 foot-pounds of work, that is, the block's weight times the distance it moves. When the block is placed on an incline of 44.5°, the force (F) needed to pull the block is reduced to 70 percent of the block's weight. While this makes the block easier to move, it must now be pulled along 43 feet of ramp to get it to a height of 30 feet. In other words, the mechanical advantage is the result of resistance, 30 feet, divided by effort, 43 feet.

Forces acting on a screw

As a screw turns, its threads exert a powerful force on the material it pierces. This force acts to pull the screw forward if it is turning clockwise and backward if it is turning counterclockwise.

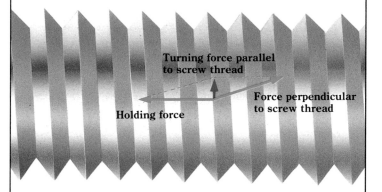

Turning force parallel to screw thread

Force perpendicular to screw thread

Holding force

A vise combines the functions of the screw and the lever.

A screw for lifting

The jackscrew exploits the great forces generated by rotating screws to lift heavy objects such as cars and trucks. By turning the central screw with the help of a lever, the two ends of the jack draw together, producing the necessary lift.

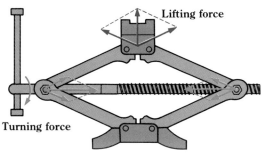

Lifting force

Turning force

Inclined planes for splitting

A wedge consists of two inclined planes joined back to back. When pounded into a piece of wood, the planes exert lateral forces sufficient to split even the strongest lumber.

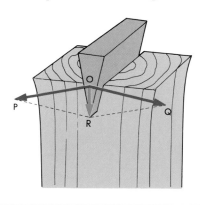

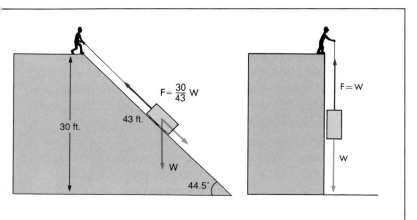

$F = \frac{30}{43} W$

30 ft.

43 ft.

W

44.5°

F = W

W

Why Do Bicycles Have Gears?

When the ancients turned the lever in a circle around a fulcrum, they discovered another of the simple machines: the wheel and axle. The bicycle uses this principle in the pedal and sprocket. The effort exerted on the rotating pedals turns the sprocket, or chainwheel gear, which connects to a chain that turns another wheel and axle, the freewheel gear attached to the rear wheel. The rider's pedaling force propels the bicycle forward at a faster speed than a person on foot could achieve with the same amount of effort.

Riders can pedal more easily, or increase the mechanical advantage of the wheel and axle, by using a series of gears of different sizes, which magnify or diminish the forces that act on them. Cyclists adjust the gear ratio—the ratio of the size of the chainwheel gear to the freewheel gear—to suit the terrain. When the freewheel gear is smaller than the chainwheel gear, the bike is harder to pedal, but the bike goes faster. A larger freewheel gear allows for easier pedaling, but the bike moves more slowly.

Freewheel   **Derailleur**

Gear ratios

By using different gear ratios, a cyclist can adjust to varying riding conditions. A low gear ratio provides little force but easier pedaling for uphill climbs, while a high ratio offers greater force for level or downhill stretches when pedaling is easy.

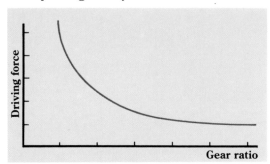

Gear ratio and driving force

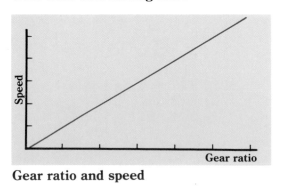

Gear ratio and speed

The freewheel gears

The smaller the freewheel gear, the more revolutions per minute the rear wheel will make with one turn of the pedals. The chart below shows the distances a bicycle travels after one revolution for five different freewheel gears.

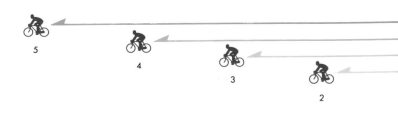

Combining gears

The chainwheel and freewheel gears vary greatly in size and number of teeth. To shift gears smoothly while in motion, multispeed bicycles use devices called derailleurs that move the chain from one gear to the next.

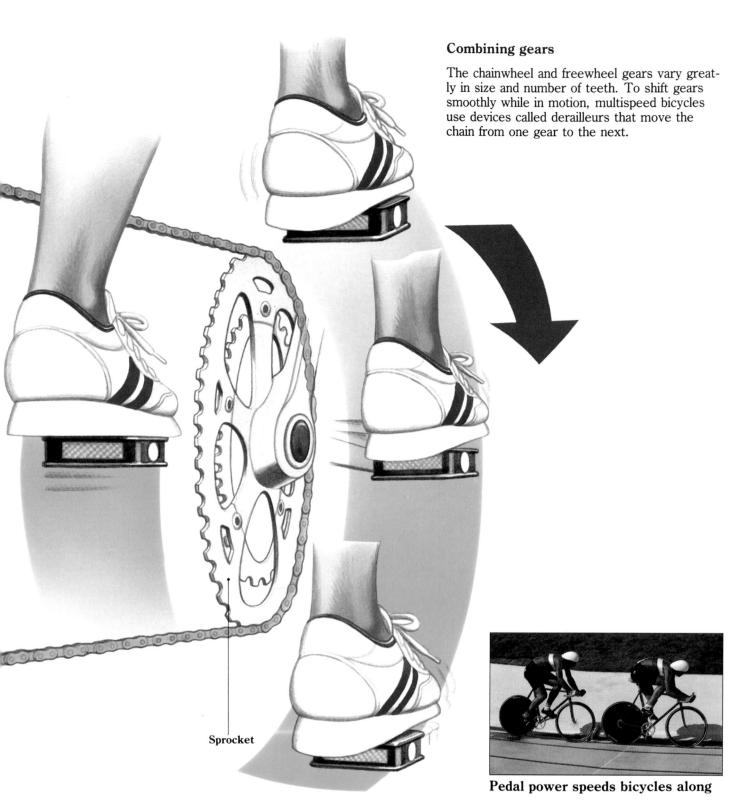

Sprocket

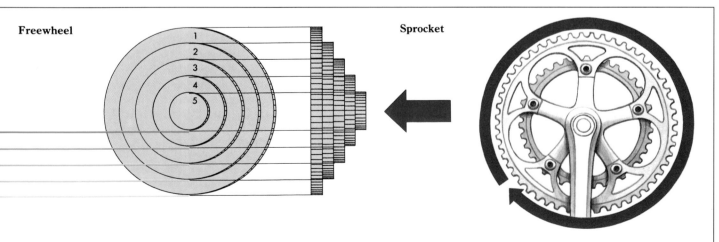

Pedal power speeds bicycles along

Freewheel

1
2
3
4
5

Sprocket

How Do Pulleys Work?

A pulley consists of a chain or a belt passed around a wheel or a series of wheels. Like the lever, a pulley reduces the effort needed to raise an object, but a pulley can also redirect the applied force. Such an advantage comes at a cost: The smaller the effort needed to lift a weight, the longer the distance through which the effort must move. A combination of pulleys multiplies the advantage by the number of weight-bearing chains used. These effort-saving devices serve many purposes, ranging from hoisting massive steel beams at construction sites to raising flags.

As with the other simple machines, the pulley's exact origins are unknown. Although they may have existed much earlier, pulleys were first documented in the fifth century BC, when the ancient Greeks used them in ships and theaters.

A fixed pulley atop a flagpole makes it easy to raise a flag by pulling down on the line to which the flag is attached.

Single fixed pulleys

The simplest type of pulley does not decrease the effort needed to raise an object but instead redirects the applied force, as at right and above right.

Rail-mounted movable pulley systems *(left)* are popular on assembly lines because they make it easy to move heavy parts. The applied force (F) equals a fraction of the number (n) of supporting chains used times the weight (W).

$F = \frac{1}{n}W$

Single fixed pulley

$F = W$

Single movable pulley

$F = \frac{1}{2}W$

Multiple pulleys

$F = \frac{1}{2}W$

Single movable pulleys

When allowed to move, a single pulley *(above)* cuts in half the effort required to raise an object. But applying half the force means the object will have to be moved twice as far, or force equals half the weight ($F = \frac{1}{2}W$).

Multiple pulleys

By using a combination of fixed and moving pulleys *(above)*, the applied force is multiplied by the total number of weight-bearing chains used, or force equals half the weight ($F = \frac{1}{2}W$).

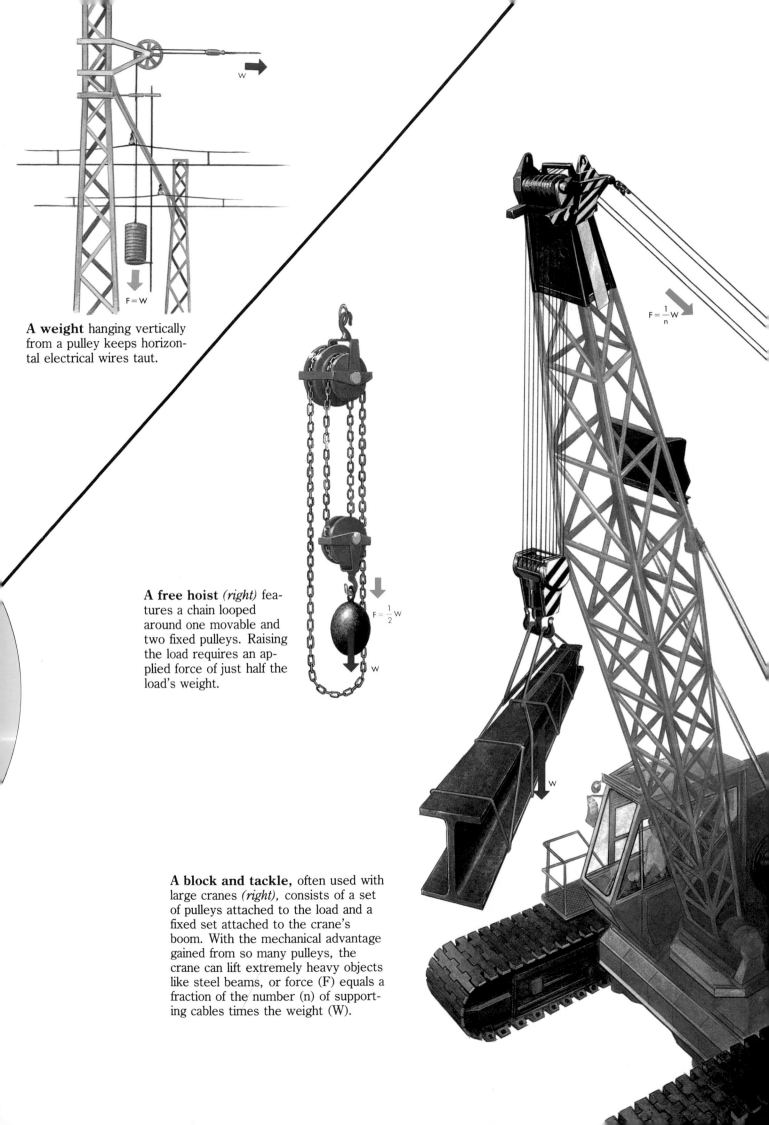

A weight hanging vertically from a pulley keeps horizontal electrical wires taut.

$$F = W$$

A free hoist *(right)* features a chain looped around one movable and two fixed pulleys. Raising the load requires an applied force of just half the load's weight.

$$F = \frac{1}{2} W$$

A block and tackle, often used with large cranes *(right),* consists of a set of pulleys attached to the load and a fixed set attached to the crane's boom. With the mechanical advantage gained from so many pulleys, the crane can lift extremely heavy objects like steel beams, or force (F) equals a fraction of the number (n) of supporting cables times the weight (W).

$$F = \frac{1}{n} W$$

How Can Springs Measure Forces?

Springs are mechanical devices that stretch and compress according to a simple law. First formulated in 1678 by English physicist Robert Hooke, this law, appropriately called Hooke's law, states that springs deform proportionally to the forces acting on them. Simply put, the greater the force pulling or pushing on a spring, the farther the spring will stretch or compress. Beyond a certain point known as the elastic limit, the bonds that link the spring's atoms will shift and permanently distort the spring, which will never recoil again.

The elasticity of springs makes them useful in scales and balances. A comparison between how much a spring is stretched by an unknown weight and a known weight makes it easy to calculate the unknown weight.

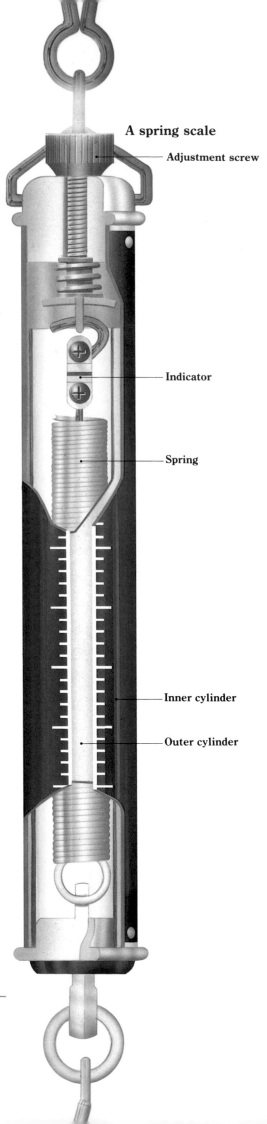

A spring scale

Adjustment screw

Indicator

Spring

Inner cylinder

Outer cylinder

Springs and forces

A spring will always stretch the same distance when subjected to the same force. If the person applying a force (F) and the block applying a weight (W) stretch the spring equally far, the force must equal the weight.

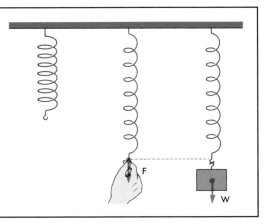

F

W

The bounce in a spring

Pulling and releasing a weight attached to a spring will generate the curve shown below; red arrows indicate the spring force and green arrows the weight. If it were not for friction, which slows these motions, the springs would stretch and compress forever.

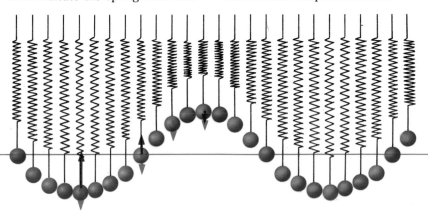

How a spring stretches

An ordinary coil spring is a torsion spring. As a force is applied to the spring and the spring stretches, the wire twists. This twisting strains the bonds that connect the individual atoms within the spring, changing the distance between the atoms. As soon as the distorting force is removed, atoms return to their original positions, restoring the spring to its original shape.

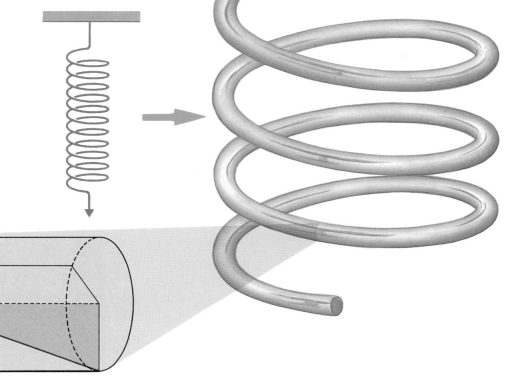

Elasticity

The atoms in a metal spring act as if they were connected by springs. When compressed, the atoms' tendency is to push back to their normal position. When driven apart, they tend to pull back toward each other, restoring the metal's original shape. If the atoms stretch beyond their elastic limit, the bonds connecting them break, and the metal is bent permanently in a new shape.

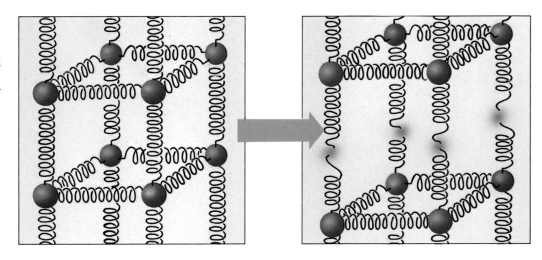

Torsion and bar springs

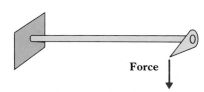

Torsion springs consist of twistable rods that revert to their original shape when released.

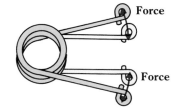

Helical springs work in shears by pushing the blades apart when pressure on the grips is released.

The most common helical spring can be found in objects such as ballpoint pens and shock absorbers.

A flat spring simply consists of a bar that flattens out again after having been bent.

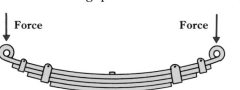

Made of several arched metal bars, leaf springs are similar to flat springs, only much stronger.

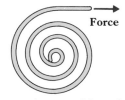

Coil springs, often used in wrist watches, can be wound tightly and fit in small spaces.

4
Temperature, Heat, and Molecules

In everyday terms, temperature, as measured by a thermometer, indicates the relative warmth or coolness of things. In scientific terms, temperature is a measure of the average kinetic energy of a substance's molecules. This kinetic energy reflects how fast the molecules move. In water at 50° C., or 122° F., the water molecules have more kinetic energy and are moving faster than the molecules in water at 5° C., or 41° F.

Although thermal energy and heat energy are often spoken of interchangeably, they are not the same thing. Thermal energy, as measured with a thermometer, is the amount of energy a substance has because its molecules are moving. Heat energy is a measure of the sum total of the energies of all its molecules. For example, a 2-pound block of ice contains twice the heat energy of a 1-pound block of ice, even though their temperatures are the same.

This chapter will show how heat can move from a warmer substance to a cooler one or through fluids such as water and air. But heat does more than travel. At 0° C., or 32° F., heat changes solid ice to liquid water. At 100° C., or 212° F.—the temperature at which water boils—heat changes liquid water to the gas called water vapor. Nearly all other substances also undergo such changes at their own distinctive temperatures. Each of these transformations—called a phase change, or a change in the state of matter—is caused by heat.

Molecular organization is the difference between ice, liquid water, and water vapor. In ice *(right),* slow-moving molecules are tightly bonded. Heat loosens these bonds *(middle),* melting the ice; more heat frees the molecules as gas *(far right).*

Why Does Ice Stay Cold As It Melts?

When ice is placed in a pot on a stove and the heat is turned on, the pot gets warm and the ice begins to melt. But as long as there is ice in the water, the water's temperature never rises above 0° C., or 32° F., no matter how hot the burner gets. That's because all of the heat goes into the ice to break the physical forces that bind water molecules together as ice.

The water molecules in ice are held together by weak bonds that form between a hydrogen atom *(blue)* on one water molecule and the oxygen atom *(red)* of another water molecule. The resulting hexagonal crystal structure is fairly strong. At 0° C., the molecules move enough so that the bonds weaken. Some of the bonds break, allowing water molecules to escape the ice as liquid. This melting process is called a phase change—water changes from its solid phase to its liquid phase—and the temperature at which it occurs is called the melting point.

Breaking the bonds that hold water together as ice requires energy—so much energy that all of the burner's heat goes into severing those bonds instead of into raising the ice's temperature. The heat needed to complete the phase change is called the latent heat of fusion or heat of transformation, as it does not cause the temperature to rise. Only when the last bonds break and the ice is melted does the water temperature rise above 0° C.

2 **When more heat** is added, water molecules at the surface of the ice vibrate faster, breaking some of the bonds holding them in place. These molecules escape from the ice as liquid water. More heat will break the remaining bonds and melt the rest of the ice.

How ice melts
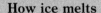

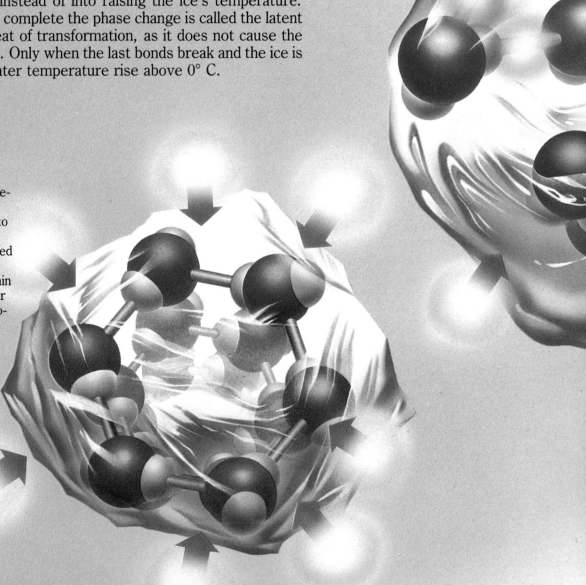

1 **In ice,** water molecules move so slowly that they bond to one another, forming a solid. When ice is heated *(yellow balls represent heat),* the molecules gain energy and move faster but are still fastened together as ice.

Water molecules

Oxygen atom

Hydrogen atom

Hydrogen atom

3 **Continued** heating finally gives the last of the molecules in the frozen water enough energy to escape the bonds that held them together as ice. All of the water is now liquid.

Temperature

Water and ice

Water

Ice

Ice, water, and temperature

Heating ice *(left)* at first raises its temperature. But at 0° C., or 32° F., a phase change begins: The ice starts to melt. As the blue graph line shows, add-ing heat melts more ice but does not raise the water temperature. Only when the ice is melted does added heat raise the water temperature *(above)*.

Heat added

How Is Extreme Heat Measured?

Measuring the temperature of a roasting turkey is a simple matter of sticking a thermometer into the bird. But trying the same approach with molten iron straight from a blast furnace, at temperatures exceeding 1,500° C., or 2,732° F., yields nothing more than a melted thermometer. Determining such extreme temperatures depends on measuring the radiant thermal energy that all hot objects emit.

Radiant thermal energy is infrared radiation—like light, a form of electromagnetic radiation. Though infrared radiation is invisible, special electronic devices can detect it. These detectors convert the energy of infrared radiation to an electric signal. The greater the infrared energy striking the detector, the stronger the signal.

In a thermogram, which is one type of high-temperature thermometer *(below),* the infrared detector senses the radiation from the hot object, and scanners select a series of points on the object to assess temperature distribution. A computer compares signals from the two sources and determines the temperature of the hot object. Thermograms measure temperatures up to 900° C., or 1,652° F.

Objects that are extremely hot emit visible as well as infrared radiation. An optical pyrometer of the disappearing-filament variety is able to measure temperatures up to 3,000° C., or 5,432° F., by matching a hot object's brightness to that of a tungsten light-bulb filament that is of known temperature.

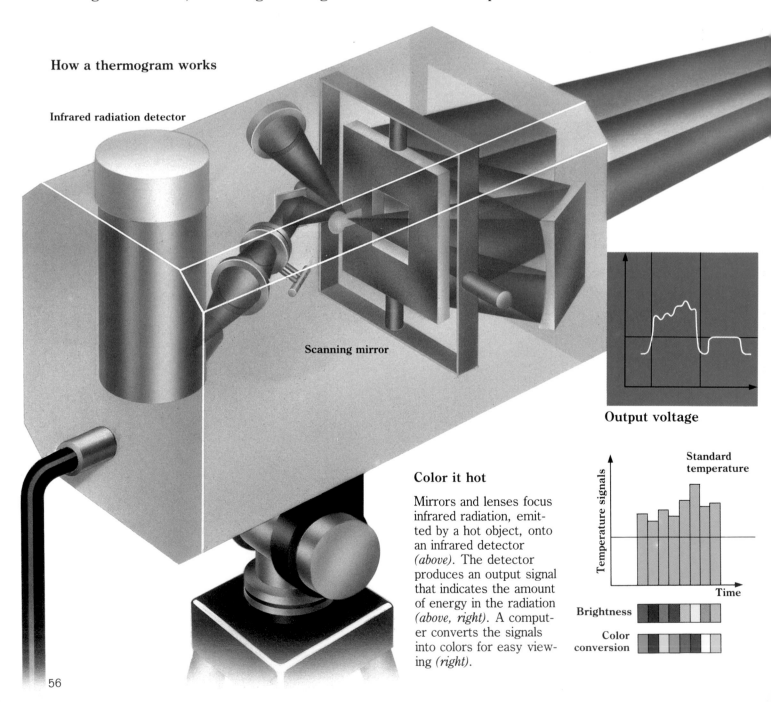

How a thermogram works

Infrared radiation detector

Scanning mirror

Output voltage

Color it hot

Mirrors and lenses focus infrared radiation, emitted by a hot object, onto an infrared detector *(above).* The detector produces an output signal that indicates the amount of energy in the radiation *(above, right).* A computer converts the signals into colors for easy viewing *(right).*

Standard temperature

Temperature signals

Time

Brightness

Color conversion

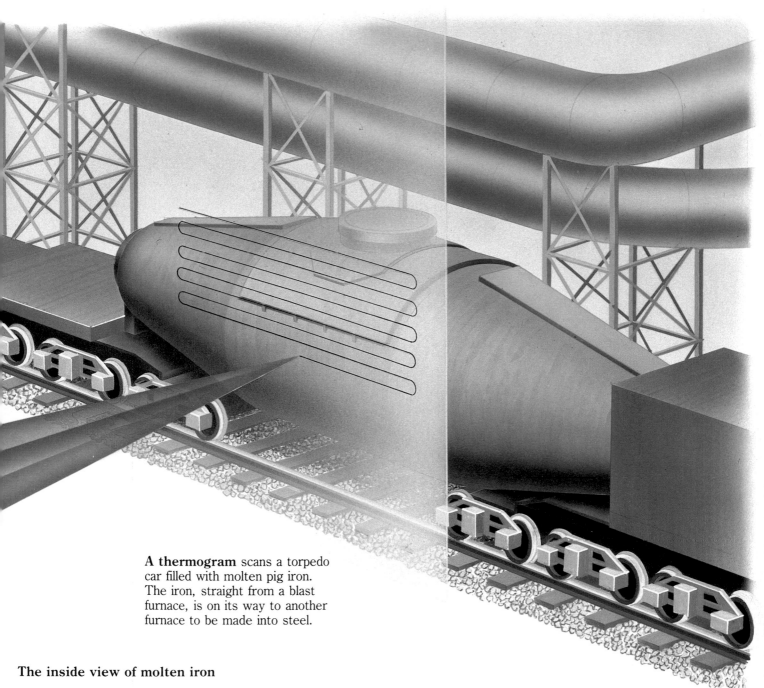

A thermogram scans a torpedo car filled with molten pig iron. The iron, straight from a blast furnace, is on its way to another furnace to be made into steel.

The inside view of molten iron

A computer assembles the output voltage signals from the thermogram *(left)* into a color-coded map of each torpedo car's temperature *(below)*. The color key on the right shows that dark blue marks the hottest areas. Four torpedo cars are temperature-mapped on this screen.

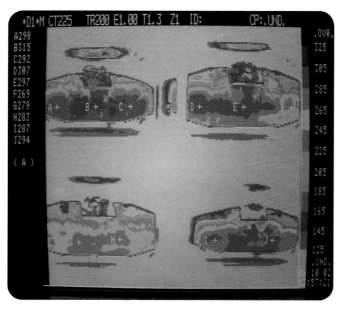

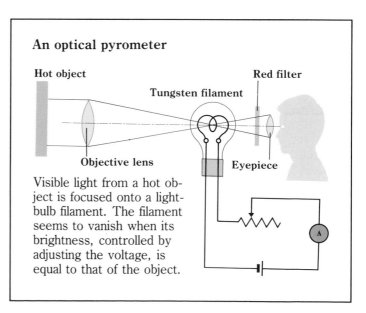

An optical pyrometer

Hot object

Tungsten filament

Red filter

Objective lens

Eyepiece

Visible light from a hot object is focused onto a light-bulb filament. The filament seems to vanish when its brightness, controlled by adjusting the voltage, is equal to that of the object.

How Does Heat Spread in Fluids?

Heating any fluid—such as water or air—forces it to expand, making it lighter. Similarly, cooling a fluid makes it contract and become heavier. The combination of these opposite physical events forms the phenomenon called convection, a process that transfers heat throughout large volumes of any liquid or gas.

When a pot of water sits on a burner *(right)*, water over the flame absorbs energy. This energy causes the water molecules to move apart from one another, making the water less dense. The warmed water *(orange column)* rises; here, the gray coloring above the flame indicates this motion. At the same time, colder, denser water *(red arrows)* sinks from the top to replace the warm water. As the hot water rises, it loses energy to the water through which it passes and cools somewhat. Meanwhile, warmer water keeps rising, pushing aside the now-cooled water. Convection stops after the flame goes out and all the water reaches the same temperature.

Convective water movement

Warmed water loses heat as it rises from the bottom of a heated beaker. At the surface, still-warmer water below pushes it aside. As it cools, the water becomes denser and sinks.

Heated water, less dense, rises

Cooled water, more dense, sinks

Added color makes the convection currents visible

A flame adds energy

Convection by heating

Heating the bottom of a test tube *(right)* warms the water there. The warm water then rises, as cooler, heavier water sinks and is heated. Eventually, all the water becomes warm. Heating the top of the tube *(below)* warms only the water at the top since warm, light water stays above cold water.

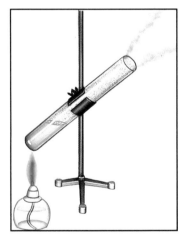

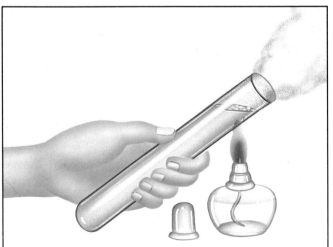

Convection in a gas

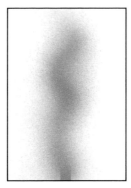  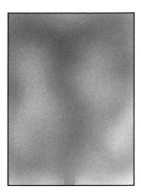

Smoke shows how convection currents form in air *(above)*. The process starts *(left)* when warm air rises in a room. When the warm air reaches the ceiling *(middle)*, it spreads outward as more warm air pushes it aside. As it loses heat, this air now sinks back to the floor. Pushed back to the heat source by cooler, trailing air *(right)*, the air is warmed and rises again.

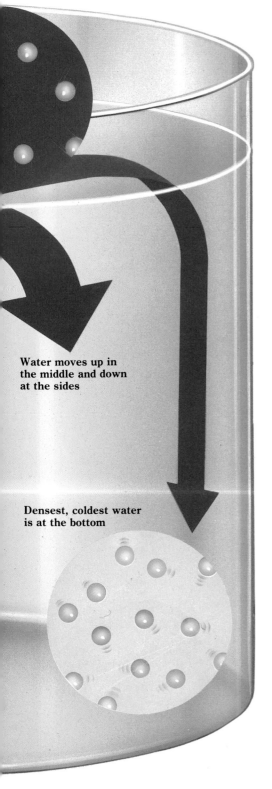

Water moves up in the middle and down at the sides

Densest, coldest water is at the bottom

Heating and cooling a room

An air conditioner cools a room most efficiently if it is near the ceiling *(top)* because cooled air *(blue)* sinks, then spreads by convection. Similarly, a heater works best when placed near the floor *(bottom)*. Warm air *(orange)* rises and then circulates in the room.

What Makes a Down Jacket So Warm?

Anyone who goes outside in cold weather without a jacket will feel chilled because the body loses heat by conduction and convection into the cooler air. But inside a down jacket, a warm body stays particularly warm. That's because down—the type of insulating feather that enables geese and ducks to stay warm while floating in cold water—has a structure that makes it difficult for the air that is next to the body to move away into colder air. When air is unable to move, it cannot carry heat away.

Heat always flows from an area that is warm to one that is cooler. A warm body loses heat when air molecules pick up energy, speed up, and move farther apart, away from warm skin. Each air molecule carries a small amount of energy. The more energy molecules take away, the colder a person feels.

Down dramatically slows heat loss by interfering with the process of convection. Each down feather has thousands of tiny hairlike projections known as barbules. The barbules of neighboring feathers interlock with one another, forming a fine net that impedes air's movement. With air motion reduced, heat convection drops as well, and the body stays warm.

How a down jacket insulates

The small feathers, or down, that fill this coat are made of thousands of tiny barbules, or hooks, growing from flexible barbs *(right)*. This structure keeps the down from clumping together and losing its insulating capacity.

Feathers. A goose has down feathers *(left)* to keep it warm, semiplumes *(middle)* to help it float, and contour feathers *(right)* to cover the others.

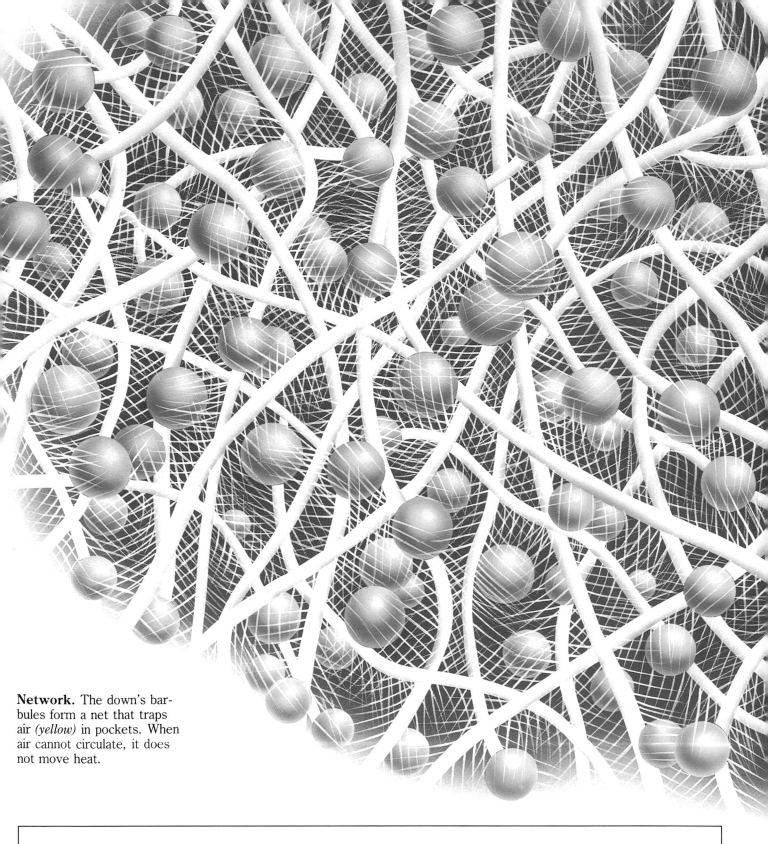

Network. The down's barbules form a net that traps
air *(yellow)* in pockets. When
air cannot circulate, it does
not move heat.

Thermal conductivity

	2	4	6	8	Units of conductivity
Air	2.4				
Cotton		4			
Wool		4			
Paper			6		
Polystyrene				8	
Iron					7200

Thermal conductivity measures how heat
flows through a substance. Down has a low
conductivity of 2.1 and insulates well; so
does air, as shown at left. By contrast, iron
conducts heat well and is a poor insulator.

Down impedes the
movement of air
(arrows), thus hold-
ing in heat and
keeping out cold.

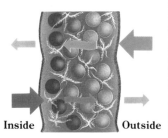

Inside   **Outside**

Why Does Boiling Water Bubble?

Any liquid, when heated, eventually reaches a temperature at which it starts boiling. Bubbles form throughout the liquid, rise to its surface, and burst, releasing hot vapor into the air. Water boils at 100° C., or 212° F. At the boiling point, every molecule has enough energy to overcome the forces holding it together with other molecules as a liquid. A pot of boiling water, for example, is full of liquid water that is turning into water vapor. At the surface, the water vapor merely escapes the boiling liquid. Beneath the surface, however, water vapor forms bubbles, each containing billions of water molecules, that rise to the top of the water.

Water that is boiling is undergoing a phase change, from the liquid to the gaseous state, in a process called vaporization. Liquids also vaporize at temperatures below the boiling point in a process called evaporation. But evaporation takes place only at the surface at the point when molecules have enough energy to escape the liquid state. While evaporation occurs more quickly when temperatures are higher, only boiling produces bubbles.

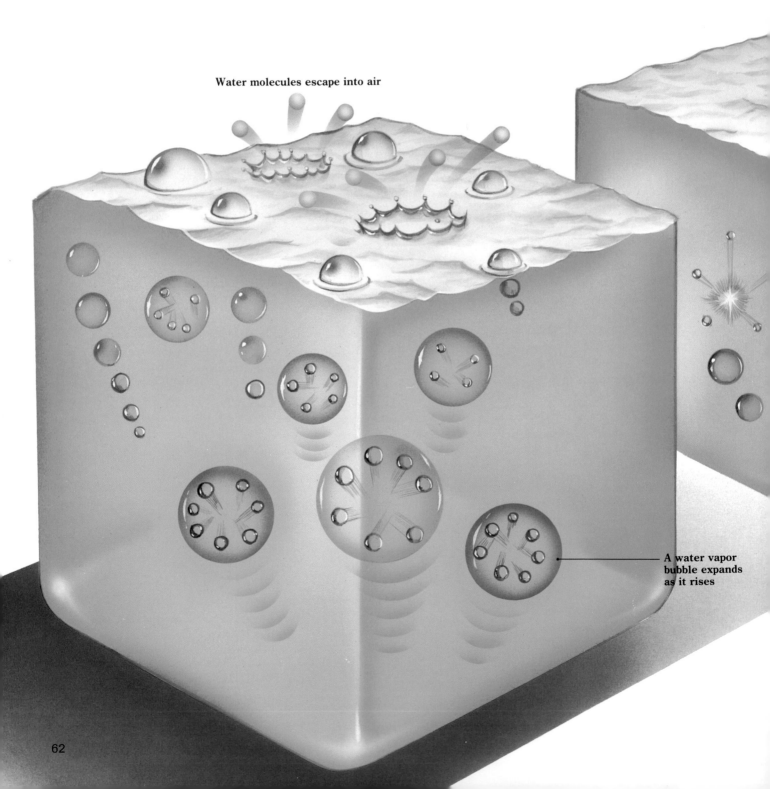

Water molecules escape into air

A water vapor bubble expands as it rises

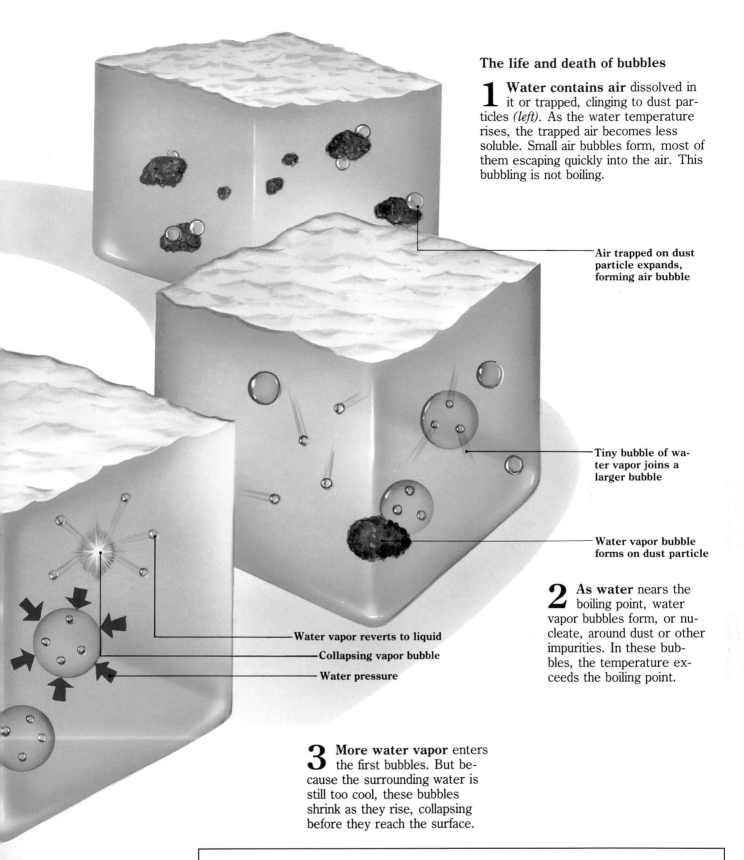

The life and death of bubbles

1 **Water contains air** dissolved in it or trapped, clinging to dust particles *(left)*. As the water temperature rises, the trapped air becomes less soluble. Small air bubbles form, most of them escaping quickly into the air. This bubbling is not boiling.

Air trapped on dust particle expands, forming air bubble

Tiny bubble of water vapor joins a larger bubble

Water vapor bubble forms on dust particle

2 **As water** nears the boiling point, water vapor bubbles form, or nucleate, around dust or other impurities. In these bubbles, the temperature exceeds the boiling point.

Water vapor reverts to liquid
Collapsing vapor bubble
Water pressure

3 **More water vapor** enters the first bubbles. But because the surrounding water is still too cool, these bubbles shrink as they rise, collapsing before they reach the surface.

4 **Bubbles form** anywhere in the boiling water. These bubbles grow larger as they rise to the surface. There they burst, and water vapor escapes into the atmosphere.

A stone to prevent eruption

In laboratory use, distilled water and other pure liquids, being dust free, offer no place for bubbles to nucleate. In such liquids, a big, sheetlike vapor bubble can form, spilling boiling liquid out of the pot in a dangerous eruption. A boiling stone, pocked with tiny holes *(right)*, prevents eruption by providing places for bubbles to form gradually.

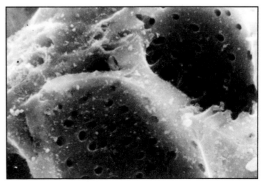

Why Doesn't Skin Burn in a Sauna?

In a sauna, the hot, dry air warms the skin immediately but does not burn it. The temperature in a sauna is close to 100° C., or 212° F., the boiling point of water at sea level, which seems hot enough to burn the skin. Indeed, spilling boiling water on the skin would cause a burn. Yet the sauna is a pleasant, not hazardous, experience.

The reason a sauna is safe is that the air inside it has very little moisture. The skin becomes warm in the sauna because energetic air molecules collide with the skin, transferring energy and raising the skin's temperature. But as the skin warms up, it begins to sweat, which is the body's mechanism for maintaining a safe temperature. In the sauna's dry air, sweat evaporates rapidly, taking heat energy with it. If the sauna's air were humid, the skin could not sweat efficiently and would stand a good chance of burning.

The same principle holds when boiling water strikes skin. In nearly constant contact with the hot water's energetic molecules, the skin has no chance to cool off by sweating. The temperature soars quickly and the skin burns.

Water vapor and sweat vapor

When the skin is cooler than the sauna's air, water vapor in the sauna *(blue arrows)* condenses on the skin, and the skin gains heat. If the skin gains too much heat, it sweats, and sweat evaporating *(purple arrows)* from the skin cools it. Balancing these two processes protects the skin.

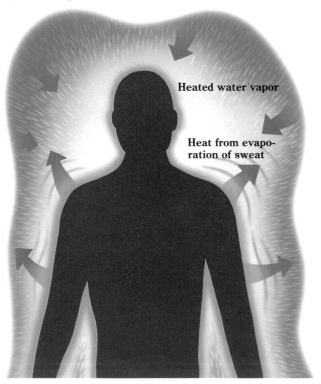

Heated water vapor

Heat from evaporation of sweat

Keeping a balance

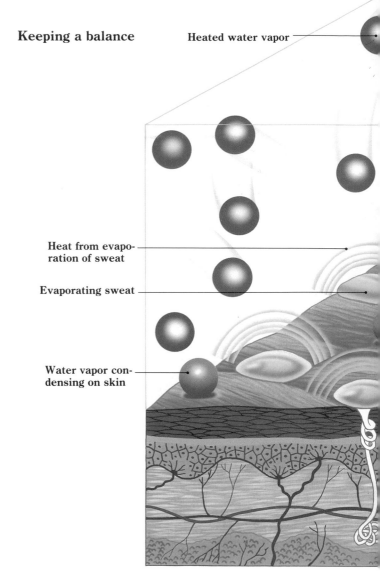

Heated water vapor

Heat from evaporation of sweat

Evaporating sweat

Water vapor condensing on skin

How water vapor transfers heat

A beaker of hot water sits near a beaker of cold water. The hot water evaporates, losing heat in this phase change and releasing many water vapor molecules. Some of these move to where water vapor molecules are less numerous, above the cold water. When they meet the cold water, they condense. This phase change adds energy to the cold water, raising its temperature. Movement continues until the beakers have the same temperature.

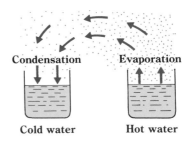

Condensation   Evaporation

Cold water   Hot water

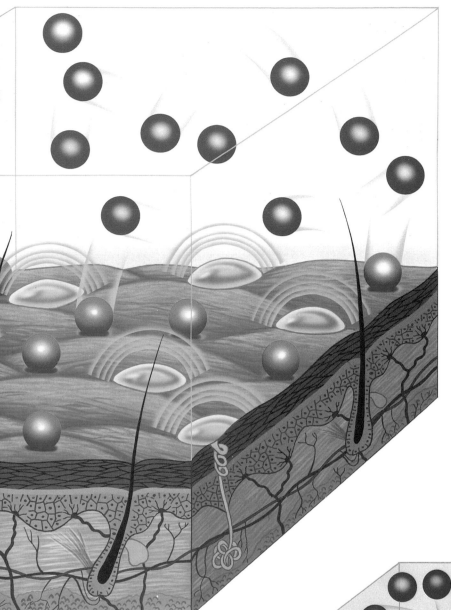

How low humidity protects skin

When the humidity in a sauna is low, as in the diagram at left, the skin can maintain a safe temperature and keep from burning. At low humidity, only a few energetic water-vapor molecules *(blue globes)* are present to collide with the skin and condense on it, transferring heat energy to the skin. Thus, the skin absorbs relatively little heat from the dry sauna air. In addition, the low humidity enables the skin to lose excess heat by sweating. As the sweat evaporates from the skin's surface, the departing water vapor molecules take heat energy with them, cooling the skin in the process.

How high humidity burns skin

If the air in a sauna is too humid *(below)*, the skin has more trouble regulating its temperature and can suffer burns. At extremely high humidity, many energetic water vapor molecules strike the skin and transfer energy to it. Thus, the skin gains heat more quickly in a moist sauna than in a dry one. And in this more humid air, sweat cannot evaporate as quickly and the skin stays hot longer.

Heating food in a steamer

Food warms evenly in a steamer *(below)* because the hot water vapor can reach it from all sides and condenses only on objects that are cooler than the steam. The cooler the item is, the more steam condenses on it, and the faster it heats.

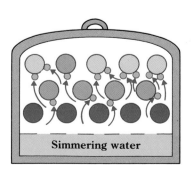

Simmering water

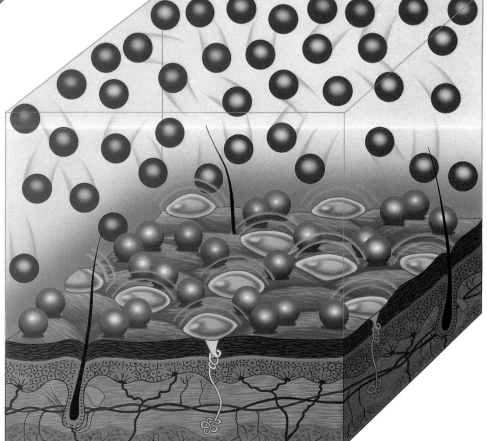

Why Does Water Freeze from the Top?

An early sign of winter is ice floating on ponds and lakes. That may not seem unusual or important, but if water acted like almost every other liquid, no one could ever skate on a pond because the ice would sink to the bottom as it formed. What's worse, the Earth would probably be a desert, with most of its water lying frozen at the bottoms of oceans, lakes, and streams.

Most liquids contract as they cool, shrinking in volume and growing denser. Solid candle wax, for example, sinks to the bottom of a pan of hotter, melted wax. Water contracts, too, but only until it reaches 4° C., or 39° F. Below that temperature, water begins to expand and its density drops. Ice is therefore lighter than near-freezing water, and as a result, it floats.

How water freezes

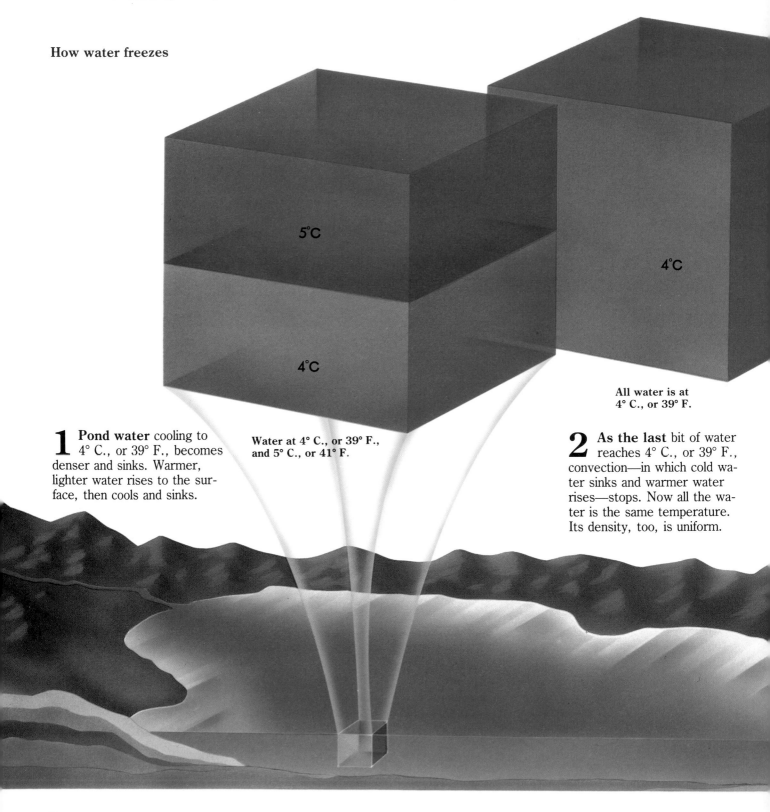

All water is at 4° C., or 39° F.

Water at 4° C., or 39° F., and 5° C., or 41° F.

1 **Pond water** cooling to 4° C., or 39° F., becomes denser and sinks. Warmer, lighter water rises to the surface, then cools and sinks.

2 **As the last** bit of water reaches 4° C., or 39° F., convection—in which cold water sinks and warmer water rises—stops. Now all the water is the same temperature. Its density, too, is uniform.

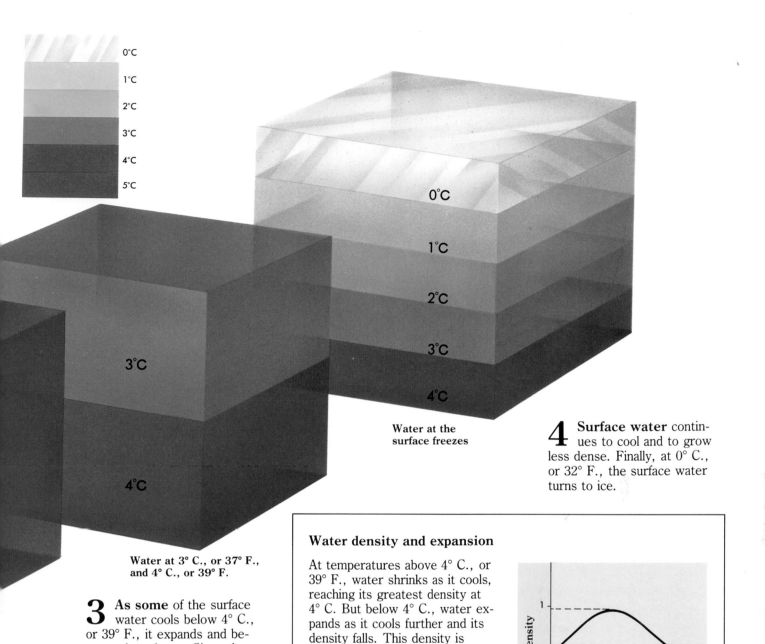

| 0°C |
| 1°C |
| 2°C |
| 3°C |
| 4°C |
| 5°C |

0°C

1°C

2°C

3°C

4°C

Water at the surface freezes

3°C

4°C

Water at 3° C., or 37° F., and 4° C., or 39° F.

3 **As some** of the surface water cools below 4° C., or 39° F., it expands and becomes less dense. Since the water at 3° C., or 37° F., is lighter than at 4° C., the cooler water stays on top.

4 **Surface water** continues to cool and to grow less dense. Finally, at 0° C., or 32° F., the surface water turns to ice.

Water density and expansion

At temperatures above 4° C., or 39° F., water shrinks as it cools, reaching its greatest density at 4° C. But below 4° C., water expands as it cools further and its density falls. This density is measured in terms of mass per unit volume, or g/cm^3.

Density

1

0

4 Temperature

Lake temperature and seasons

In summer, water is warmer at the surface than below. In winter, the top may freeze, but the bottom is warmer.

Wax and ice freeze differently

A bump forms on an ice cube *(below, left)* because the water at the center, freezing last and expanding as it freezes, can only rise. But a dip forms in the top of a wax block, because wax *(below, center)* contracts after it solidifies. Liquids that contract evenly as they freeze *(below, right)* form a curved surface.

Change in volume

Temperature

Freezing point

Wax loses volume after it freezes.

Original surface of liquid

| Ice | Wax | |

5
Electricity and Magnetism

Although electricity and magnetism seem mysterious, they can be found in the most ordinary places—everywhere, in fact, that matter exists. They dwell unseen in the atoms that compose all things. The carriers of electric and magnetic forces are charged particles—the positive protons in the atom's nucleus and the negative electrons that, planetlike, orbit about them.

These particles are governed by a natural law in which opposite charges attract and like charges repel. Electricity and magnetism are both expressions of this fundamental principle. When a sock sticks to a sheet in the clothes dryer, static electricity—caused by a buildup of opposite charges—is to blame. When a lamp lights up, electrons flowing through a wire toward a positive charge carry the necessary energy.

Scientists have found many ways to harness electric and magnetic forces. Arising from the electric and magnetic processes found in atoms, these forces appear in various forms of energy, including current electricity and electromagnetic waves. This chapter will explore the origins and behavior of electricity and magnetism, and look at some of the clever ways scientists measure and manage these remarkable forces.

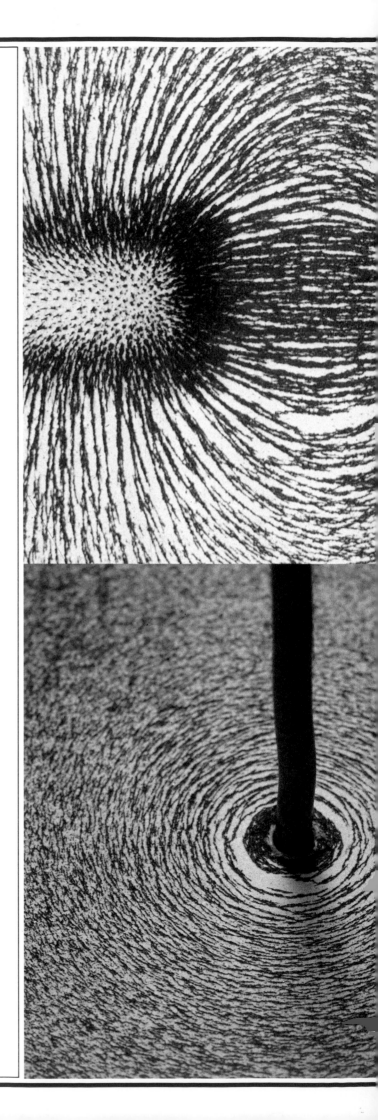

Iron filings trace the lines of magnetic force around *(counterclockwise from top)* bar magnets, an electrified wire, and a metal coil carrying electric current. The images dramatize the intimate link between the forces of electricity and magnetism.

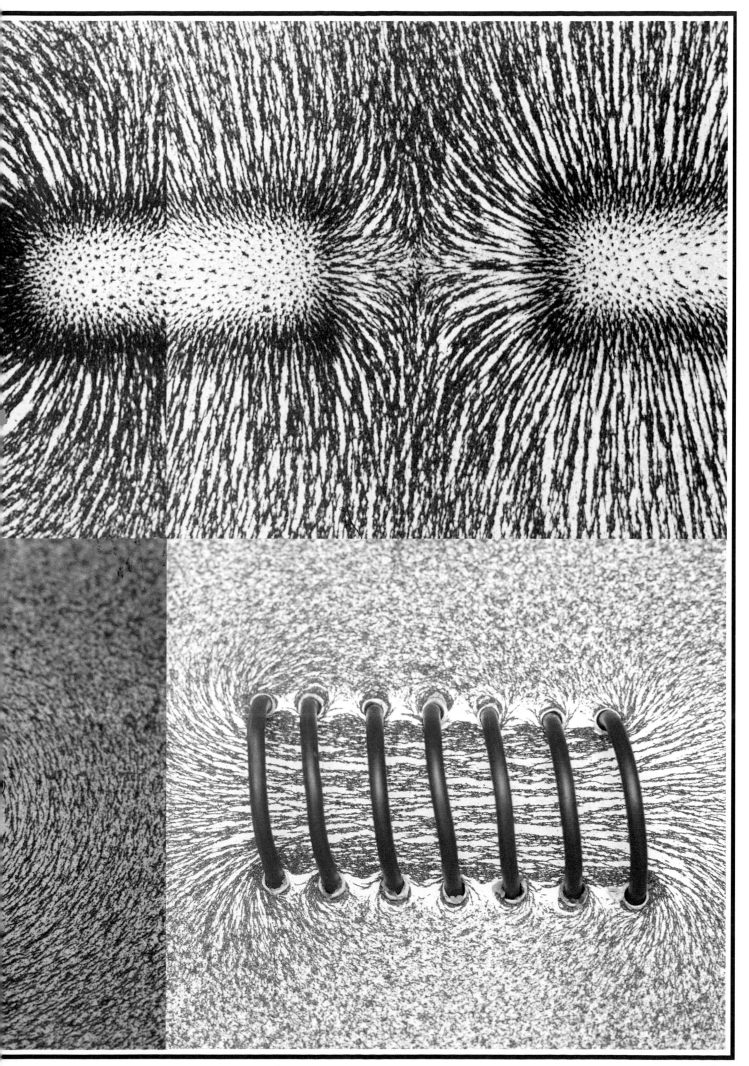

How Can Plastic Attract Paper?

Sometimes, common objects display seemingly extraordinary powers: A plastic rod may attract paper the way a magnet attracts iron or the way Styrofoam clings to things. Such small wonders are caused by static electricity.

Static electricity results from interactions between electrically charged particles—the negative electrons and the positive protons of atoms. Normally, objects are in a balanced electrical state, since they consist of an equal number of evenly distributed negative and positive particles. If they gain or lose electrons, however, these neutral objects can become charged.

Objects become charged through friction, or rubbing, which robs some substances of a portion of their electrons, leaving them with a positive charge. For example, rubbing a plastic rod across fur transfers electrons from the fur to the plastic. The plastic then has a negative charge and the fur a positive charge. If the negatively charged plastic is then brought near electrically balanced scraps of paper, the paper will stick to the plastic. The "magnetic" hold is caused by the buildup of a negative charge in the plastic.

Electricity's cardinal rule

A fundamental law of electricity states that opposite charges (+ −) attract each other, while identical charges (++ or − −) repel. The strength of these forces depends on distance: The closer the charged objects are to each other, the stronger the force.

Attraction of opposite electrical charges

Repulsion of like electrical charges

Charge without touch

If a negatively charged wand is held next to a neutral object, the charge will drive surface electrons in the object (−, *blue*) to the far side. The object's near side will become positive (+, *pink*).

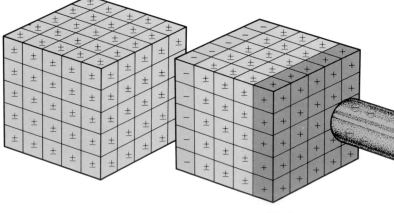

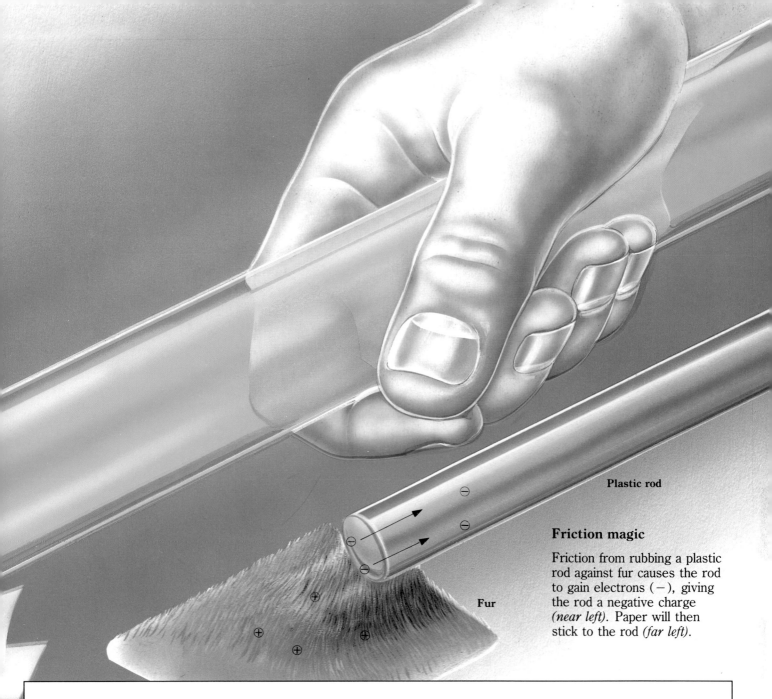

Plastic rod

Friction magic

Friction from rubbing a plastic rod against fur causes the rod to gain electrons (−), giving the rod a negative charge *(near left)*. Paper will then stick to the rod *(far left)*.

Fur

Determining charge

Certain materials have more "free" electrons that are held loosely to individual atoms (−). Others bind their electrons tightly to positive nuclei (+). When two mate-

rials such as Styrofoam and feathers are rubbed together, the one with more free electrons, feathers, will give up its loose electrons and gain a positive charge.

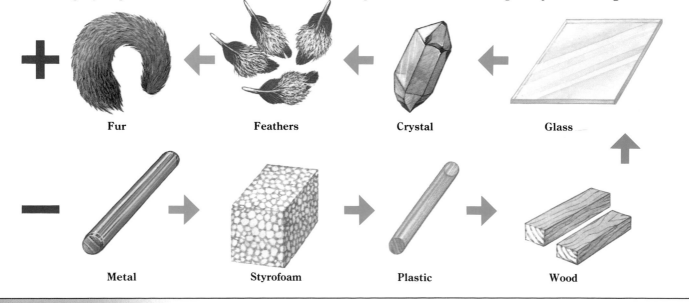

Fur	Feathers	Crystal	Glass

Metal	Styrofoam	Plastic	Wood

How Does a Light Bulb Glow?

The electricity that illuminates lamps—and that runs televisions and appliances—consists of flowing electrons, or current electricity. When a free electron is triggered to move, it occasionally will bump against an atom, exciting the atom, which means it gives some of its energy to the atom. The atom then releases this extra energy as electromagnetic radiation and propels other electrons into action. As electrons flow through the metal filament of an incandescent light bulb, the heating of the filament causes it to give off electromagnetic radiation and glow white hot.

In fluorescent lamps *(far right)*, a current flows through a gas instead of a filament. As the current travels through the gas tube, it causes the gas to give off ultraviolet energy, which excites the phosphor coating inside the tube, triggering a chain reaction that releases electromagnetic radiation as visible light.

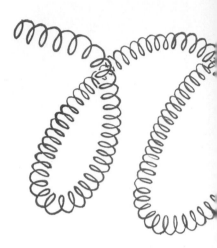

Filament

Glass support

Supporting wire

The wavelength at which hot objects emit radiation most intensely depends on the objects' temperature. The sun, at 6,000° Kelvin (K.), emits most of its radiation as visible light, while the filament of a 100-watt light bulb, at about 3,000° K., gives off most of its energy in the infrared and only a little in the visible range.

Base

Positive nucleus

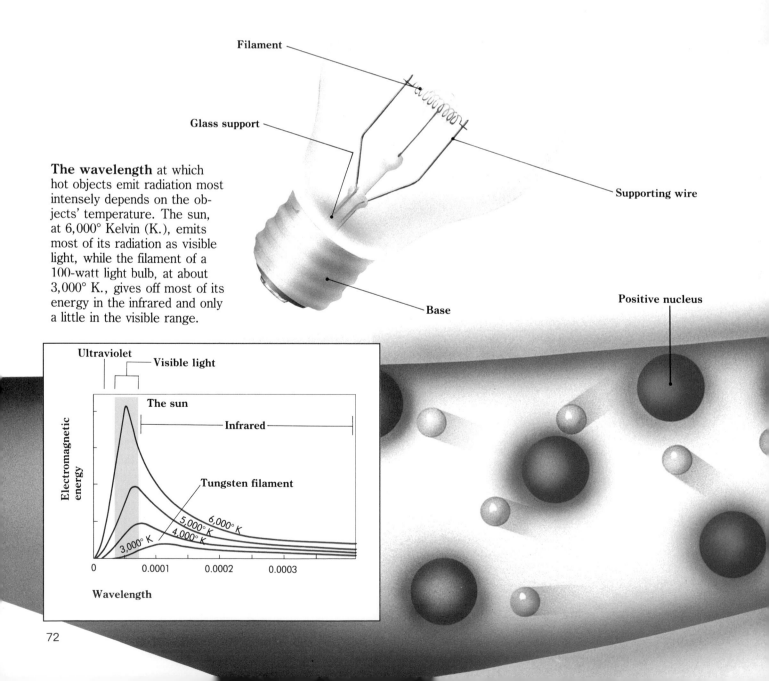

Ultraviolet

Visible light

The sun

Infrared

Electromagnetic energy

Tungsten filament

6,000° K
5,000° K
4,000° K
3,000° K

0   0.0001   0.0002   0.0003

Wavelength

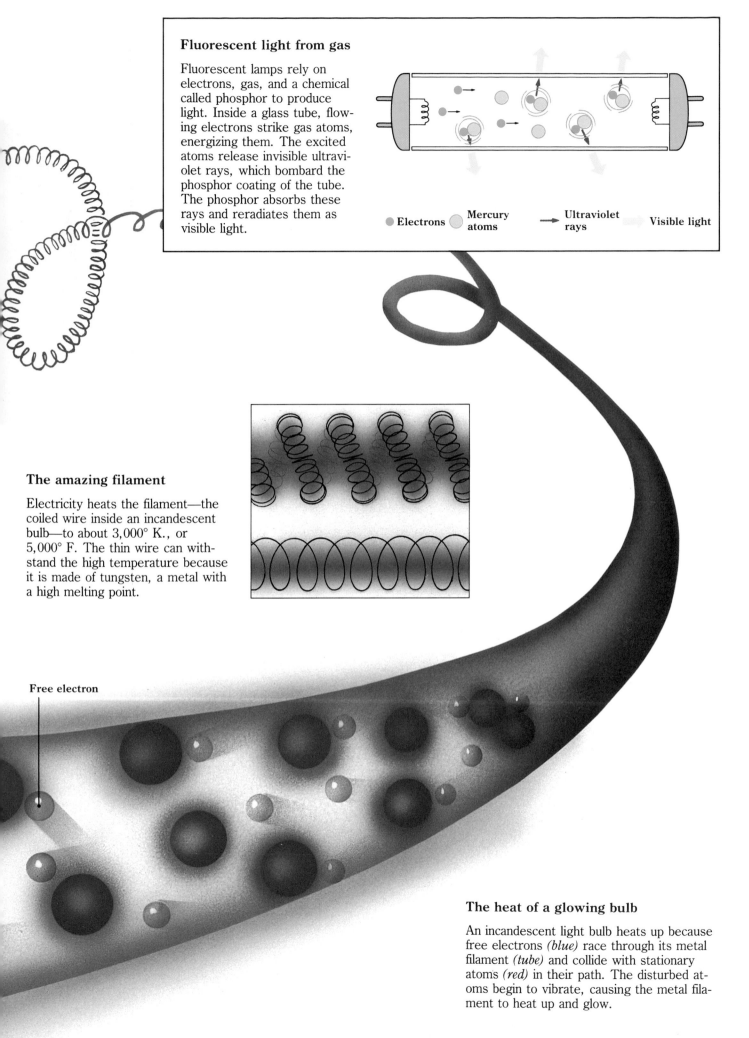

Fluorescent light from gas

Fluorescent lamps rely on electrons, gas, and a chemical called phosphor to produce light. Inside a glass tube, flowing electrons strike gas atoms, energizing them. The excited atoms release invisible ultraviolet rays, which bombard the phosphor coating of the tube. The phosphor absorbs these rays and reradiates them as visible light.

● Electrons   Mercury atoms   → Ultraviolet rays   Visible light

The amazing filament

Electricity heats the filament—the coiled wire inside an incandescent bulb—to about 3,000° K., or 5,000° F. The thin wire can withstand the high temperature because it is made of tungsten, a metal with a high melting point.

Free electron

The heat of a glowing bulb

An incandescent light bulb heats up because free electrons *(blue)* race through its metal filament *(tube)* and collide with stationary atoms *(red)* in their path. The disturbed atoms begin to vibrate, causing the metal filament to heat up and glow.

How Does Electricity Work?

Electric and water currents

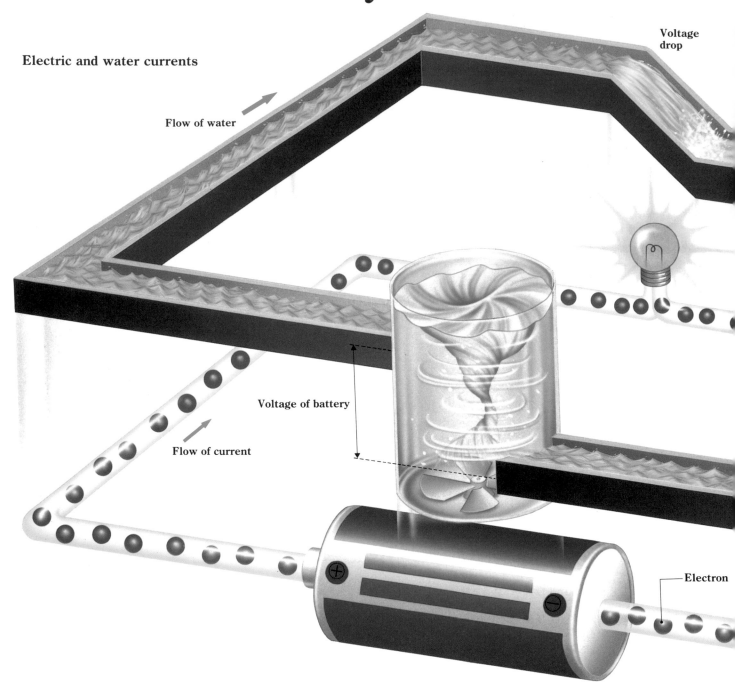

Voltage drop

Flow of water

Voltage of battery

Flow of current

Electron

Electric current can run machinery only when it is harnessed in a circuit. A circuit is a channel through which electricity moves. Its source is a power supply, such as a battery, to which an appliance like a lamp is connected by a power cord.

The circuit does not end in the appliance but loops back to the power source. The power that keeps the electric current flowing in a circuit is known as the electromotive force, or voltage. Because appliances retard a circuit's current they are called resistors.

Understanding the relationship between electric current, voltage, and resistance can be made easier by imagining the current as water flowing in a duct *(above)*. The battery can be thought of as a water pump and the electric current as the volume of water. Representing the circuit's resistors—the two light bulbs—are two water slides in the duct.

In this model, each time the water (current) hits a slide (a resistor), it drops to a lower level (a lesser voltage). The volume of water stays the same, but its height (power) diminishes. So it is with electric current. When the current passes through a resistor, its energy is siphoned off and its voltage decreases.

Calculating voltage drop

When electric current passes through a resistor, such as a light bulb, the pressure, or voltage, on the current decreases. This decrease is called a voltage drop. The change in voltage can be figured mathematically by multiplying the amount of resistance by the amount of electric current.

Current and electron flow

Electrons *(blue balls)* flow toward their power source's positive pole, giving rise to a current that moves from the positive pole to the negative *(large blue arrow)*. How much current flows depends on the number of electrons traveling through in a set time.

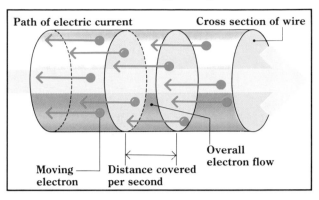

Path of electric current   **Cross section of wire**

Moving electron   **Distance covered per second**   **Overall electron flow**

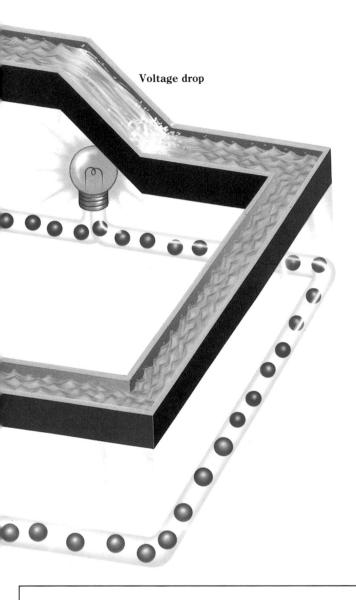

Voltage drop

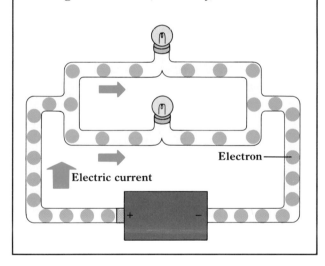

Tracing a parallel circuit

In a parallel circuit, the electric current *(blue arrows)* traces two separate paths before returning to its source *(red battery)*.

Electron

Electric current

Circuits and voltage

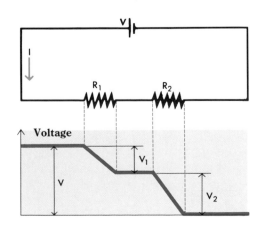

Voltage

V_1

V

V_2

The series circuit at left includes two resistors (R), which successively decrease the voltage (V). The drop in voltage is the sum of the resistance.

In a parallel circuit *(right)*, the current travels along different paths. The positions of the resistors (R) cause a simultaneous drop in voltage.

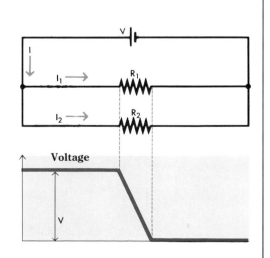

Voltage

V

How Is Electricity Measured?

Because electricity is invisible, scientists have devised ingenious ways of measuring it. One way is with the help of a galvanometer *(right),* which consists of a thin wire coil carrying current between the poles of a permanent magnet. When electricity travels along the wire coil, the current produces an electromagnetic force strong enough to move the coil past the magnet. The galvanometer gauges how much current flows through the circuit by how far the coil moves. An ammeter uses this concept with the addition of a needle and scale, which indicate the rate of current flow in amperes. By adding a resistor, the instrument becomes a voltmeter, which measures voltage, the force moving the current through the circuit.

The right-hand rule

When a current-carrying wire is in the magnetic field of a permanent magnet, the combined energy of the current and the magnetic field produces an electromagnetic force strong enough to move the wire. To remember the relationship between the direction of the current, the force, and the magnetic field, physics students devised a mnemonic called the right-hand rule. By extending the thumb of the right hand, the thumb indicates the direction of current flow; the fingers point in the direction of the external magnetic field; the palm faces the direction of the electromagnetic force.

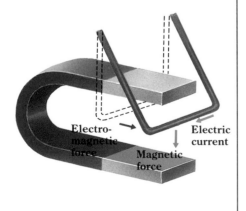

Inside an ammeter

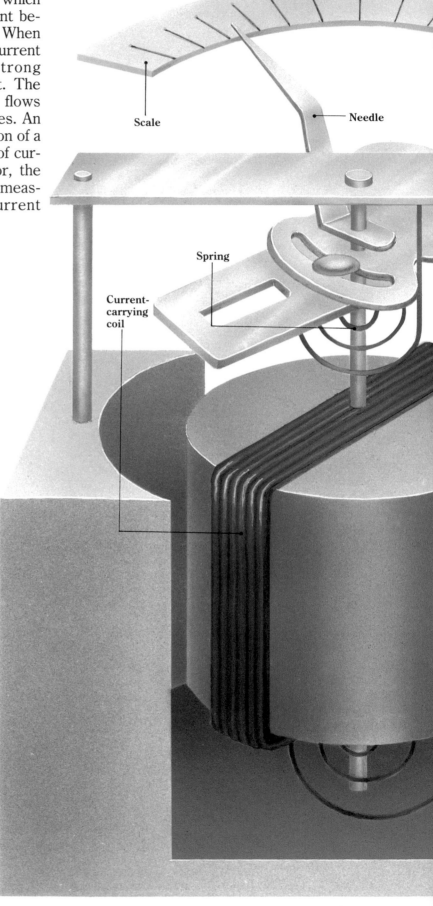

Scale

Needle

Spring

Current-carrying coil

Ammeter

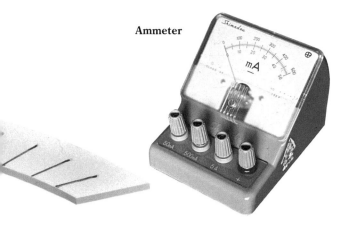

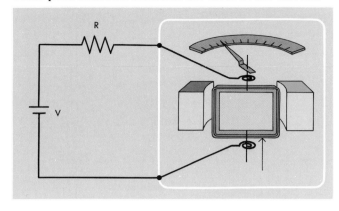

How an ammeter works

When an ammeter is connected to a circuit, the electricity generates an electromagnetic force that converts the meter's coil into a bar magnet. The permanent magnet *(pink/green boxes)* causes the bar magnet to align its north pole with the permanent magnet's south pole. A needle indicates the level of the current.

Permanent magnet

Measuring current

The electromagnetic force, generated in the coil of the ammeter, acts at right angles to the magnetic field of the permanent magnet. Since the amount of current determines the size of the magnetic force, which affects the deflection of the needle, the ammeter can measure current. The stronger the current *(far right)*, the higher the reading.

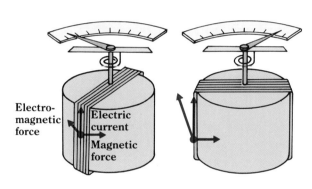

Electromagnetic force

Electric current

Magnetic force

Making a voltmeter

If an ammeter is connected to a resistor (R_V)—an object that slows the flow of electricity—then to a circuit, the instrument measures the voltage in the electric circuit. Voltage indicates the amount of force that is moving the current through a circuit.

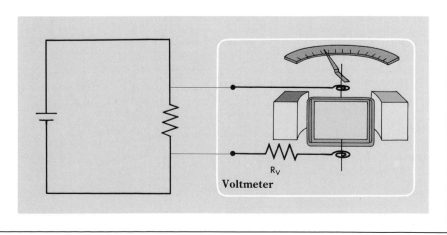

R_V

Voltmeter

Why Does a Magnet Attract Iron?

As if by magic, a magnet can attract certain metallic objects. Its power comes from the special way its electrons behave. Since an electron spinning about an atom generates a magnetic field, all atoms are tiny magnets; but in most substances, the atoms' haphazard magnetic effects cancel each other out.

In magnets, however, the atoms' magnetic fields line up in such a way that they create regions called domains. These fields have a north and a south pole. So-called field lines *(green*

lines)—concentrated regions of magnetism— run from a magnet's north pole to its south pole. This is known as the field direction. A magnet's north pole will attract another's south pole, while two identical poles will repel each other. Magnets only attract certain metals, chiefly iron, nickel, and cobalt, known as ferromagnetic materials. Though these materials are not natural magnets, their atoms rearrange themselves near a magnet so that they acquire magnetic poles.

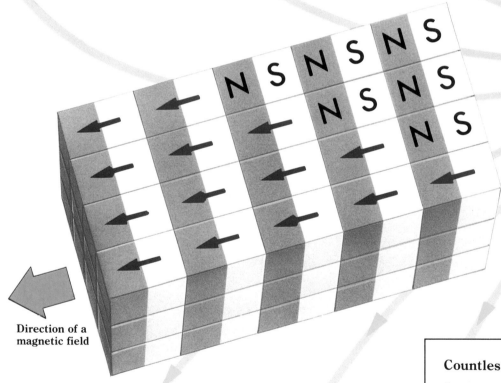

**Direction of a
magnetic field**

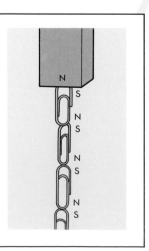

A magnetic chain

Touching the end of a magnet to metal paper clips causes each clip to develop north and south poles. The clips' poles point in the same direction as the magnet's. Each paper clip has become a magnet.

Countless tiny magnets

Some metals have a crystal structure of atoms grouped in magnetic domains. The domains' magnetic poles normally point in different directions *(red arrows)* and do not act as magnets.

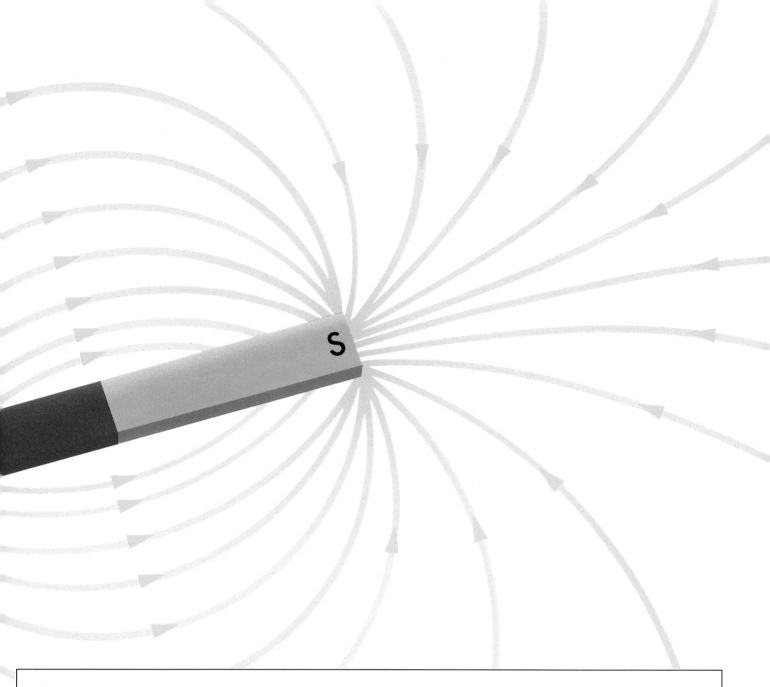

Creating a permanent magnet

1. Typically, iron's magnetic domains are randomly oriented *(pink arrows)*. This neutralizes the natural magnetism in the metal.

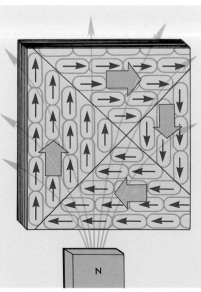

2. When a magnet *(pink bar)* is brought near, the magnetic domains in the iron begin to align with the magnet's field *(green lines)*.

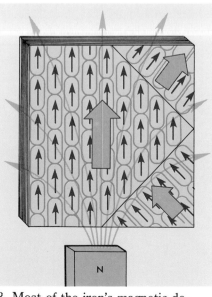

3. Most of the iron's magnetic domains quickly line up with the magnet's field. Then the iron itself becomes a permanent magnet.

How Can Electricity Make a Magnet?

The discovery that electric currents generate magnetic fields led scientists to develop a magnet using electricity that can be turned on and off. As shown at right, such electromagnets can consist of a battery attached to a coiled wire—a solenoid—wrapped around a ferromagnetic core (usually iron). The magnetic field produced by the electric current in the wire magnetizes the metal core in the same way that a permanent magnet magnetizes a piece of iron (pages 78-79).

As long as current flows through the wire, the electromagnet behaves like a permanent magnet: Magnetic field lines arc from the electromagnet's north to its south pole—usually at right angles to the flow of the current, in keeping with electromagnetic laws. If the current switches di-

rection, the magnet's poles flip and the field lines reverse as well. The overall shape of the magnetic field does not change, however. The pattern of field lines remains the same unless the shape of the wire itself changes (far right). Motors, generators, and other electrical systems operate by electromagnetism.

Electromagnet

Iron core

Iron fragments

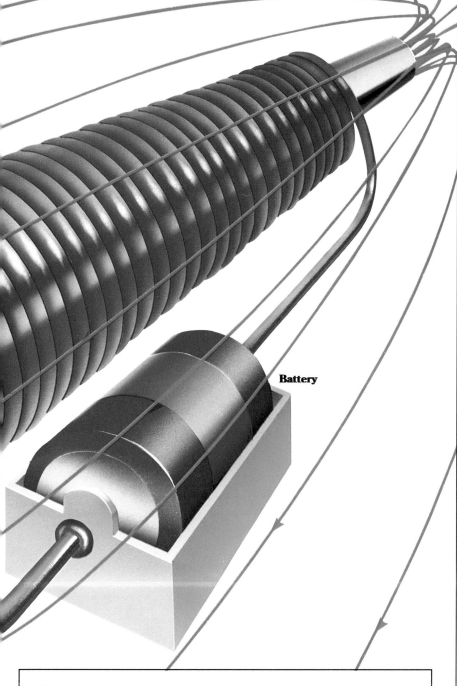

Magnetic field lines

Battery

The shape of magnetic fields

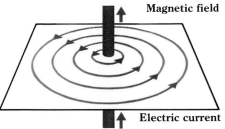

Magnetic field

Electric current

A straight-line electric current flowing upward produces concentric rings of a magnetic field that travel counter-clockwise. Reversing the current makes the field run clockwise.

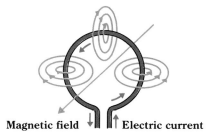

Magnetic field **Electric current**

A single electrified coil with a counterclockwise current generates magnetic field lines that run directly through the coil's open center, then up and back, forming circles.

Magnetic field and many coils

Each loop in a length of coiled, electrified wire (a solenoid) behaves like a single coil *(below)*. The pattern of a magnetic field surrounding the solenoid itself is a combination of all the individual fields created by the loops.

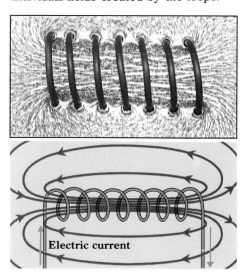

Electric current

Finding field directions

To determine the direction of magnetic field lines around a coiled electrified wire, physicists imagine gripping the wires in the direction of the electric current with the right hand. An extended thumb points in the direction of the magnetic field.

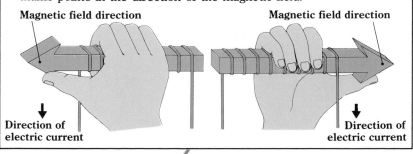

Magnetic field direction   **Magnetic field direction**

Direction of electric current   **Direction of electric current**

What Allows Electricity to Flow?

Electricity flashes through copper wire but halts when it bumps up against rubber tubing. Such examples abound in nature—certain substances are good conductors, while others block even the weakest electric current. Whether a material transmits electricity is dictated by the material's atomic structure. How easily a material channels electricity depends on how freely electrons move through it.

Conductors—chiefly metals such as iron, nickel, silver, and copper—have "loose," or free, electrons. Not leashed to any particular atom, these free electrons roam through their atomic neighborhoods, orbiting first one atom and then another. When a conductor is connected to a battery, the electric field organizes the aimless movement of the electrons into a steady flow. For this reason, metals are excellent carriers of electricity.

Insulators, however, have few, if any, free electrons. Atoms in materials such as leather, glass, plastics, and rubber keep a tight rein on their electrons. An absence of freewheeling charges keeps insulators from conducting current.

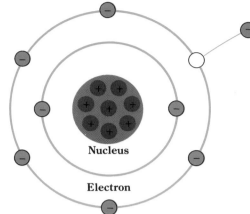

Atoms of conductors have one or more free electrons. Such electrons do not remain in fixed orbits about the nucleus but drift slowly through the surrounding atomic structure. When they move, they transmit electricity.

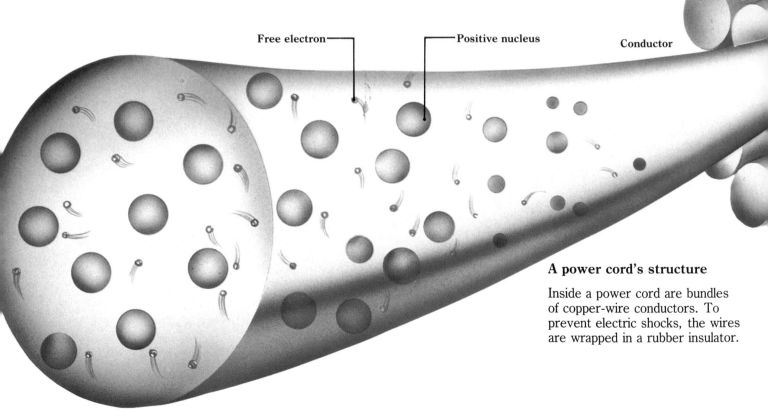

Free electron — Positive nucleus — Conductor

A power cord's structure

Inside a power cord are bundles of copper-wire conductors. To prevent electric shocks, the wires are wrapped in a rubber insulator.

Current in a conductor

When the conductor is attached to a battery *(far right)*, electrons *(blue)* begin an orderly flow toward the battery's positive terminal, creating electric current.

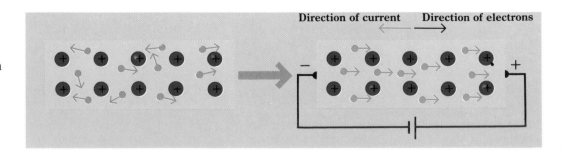

Direction of current ← Direction of electrons →

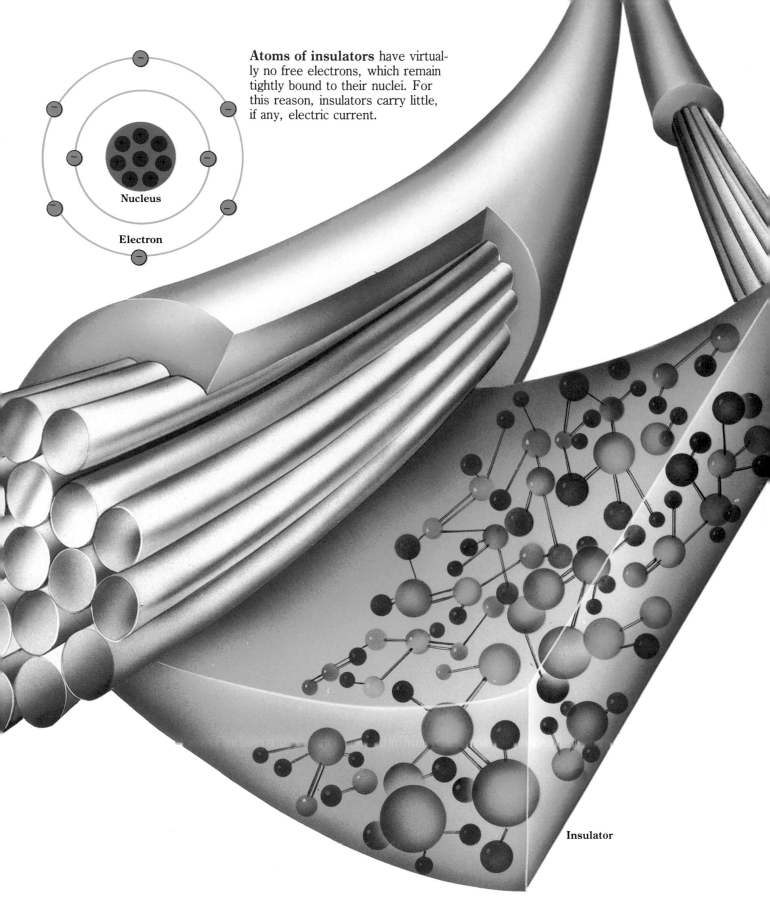

Atoms of insulators have virtually no free electrons, which remain tightly bound to their nuclei. For this reason, insulators carry little, if any, electric current.

Nucleus

Electron

Insulator

The current-free insulator

An insulator's electrons are tied to their positive nuclei. Even if the insulator is connected to a battery *(far right)*, the electrons stay in place and current does not flow through.

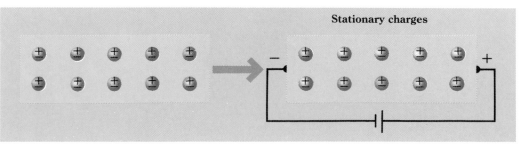

Stationary charges

What Is a Semiconductor?

A semiconductor is a crystalline material that conducts electricity but not as well as metals; it also resists electricity but not as well as many insulators. In general, semiconductors' electrons are tightly bound to their nuclei. But if a few atoms of antimony—with a surplus of electrons—are incorporated in a semiconductor such as silicon, the free electrons will give it a negative charge. By replacing a few atoms with indium, which has room for extra electrons, the semiconductor has holes where electrons should be; the holes relay a positive charge.

These properties make semiconductors useful in transistors to amplify current, to block current, or to let current flow in only one direction. In a typical NPN transistor *(opposite, top),* a layer of positive (P) semiconductor, the base, is sandwiched between two negative (N) layers, the emitter and the collector. When, for example, a small signal from an intercom is channeled through the base, the movement of electrons amplifies the signal.

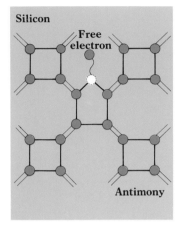

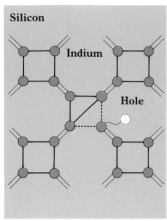

N-type   P-type

Looking into semiconductors

Negatively charged N-type semiconductors have excess electrons. Positive P-types lack electrons but have holes where electrons should be.

Intercom

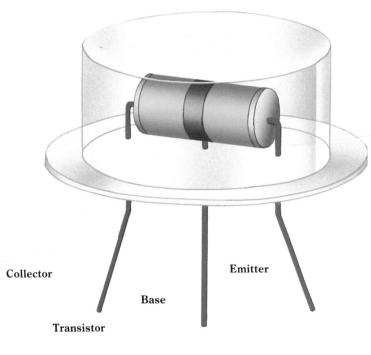

Collector

Emitter

Base

Transistor

The semiconductor difference

Unlike conductors, which have many free electrons, and insulators, which have virtually none, a semiconductor has a small number of free electrons and so-called holes *(white dot)*—empty spots left by free electrons. Both holes and electrons conduct current.

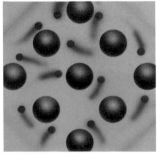

Conductor

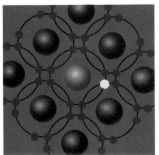

Semiconductor

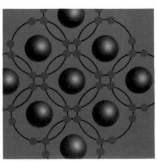

Insulator

The NPN transistor

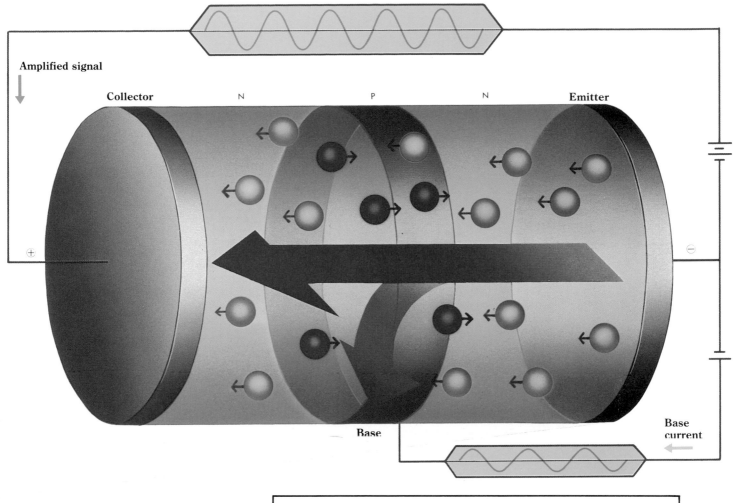

Amplified signal

Collector   N   P   N   Emitter

Base

Base current

The PNP transistor

Holes move from the positive emitter (+) to the negative base *(N-layer)* and on to the positive collector at the negative terminal (−), adding to the current.

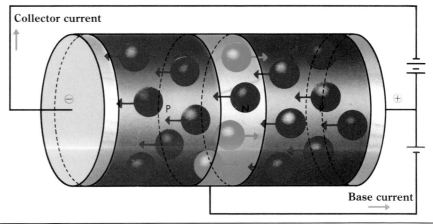

Collector current

P   N

Base current

On or off

When negatively charged electrons *(blue)* and positively charged holes *(pink)* are repelled at the junction of the N-type and P-type silicon in the diode *(near right),* current breaks. At bottom, electrons and holes are drawn toward the junction, and the diode is conducting current in one direction, converting AC current to DC.

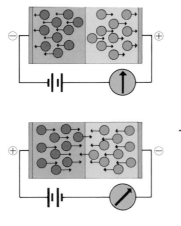

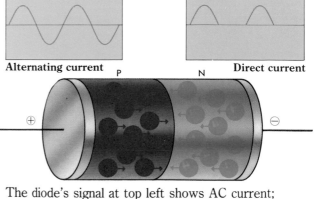

Alternating current   P   N   Direct current

The diode's signal at top left shows AC current; at top right only DC current gets through.

How Is Electricity Sent to a Home?

The electricity used in homes comes from large electric generating stations. These utilities transmit electricity to regional substations, which then distribute it to consumers.

Because transmission lines resist current flow, the current loses energy as heat. The amount of power lost depends on current flow. Direct current (DC) flows in one direction; alternating current (AC) regularly reverses its course. Years ago, utilities supplied DC current. For complex reasons, DC current transmission is hard to control, so the safety-conscious utilities transmitted it at low voltages. But by the time the DC current reached consumers, resistance had robbed it of 45 percent of its strength.

The solution was to transmit high-voltage AC current, which is easily converted by transformers *(below)*. Because high-voltage transmissions require less current for the same amount of power, they sacrifice less energy to resistance. When AC current leaves the utility, step-up transformers boost it from 22,000 to 765,000 volts, and step-down transformers reduce it to the 110 or 220 volts used in homes.

Terrific transformers

Transformers increase or decrease AC voltage. AC current enters a primary coil wrapped around an iron core. The current's back-and-forth motion sets up a changing magnetic field in the core. When the field moves from the core to the secondary coil, it generates AC current there. If the secondary coil has more loops than the primary, the output voltage will be larger than the input.

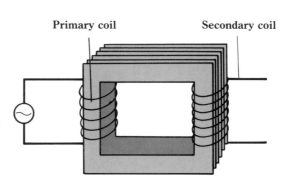

Primary coil   Secondary coil

DC power loss

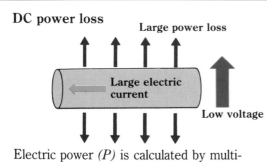

Large power loss

Large electric current

Low voltage

Small power loss

Small electric current

High voltage

Electric power *(P)* is calculated by multiplying current *(I)* times voltage *(V)*, or $P = I \times V$. As voltage increases, the current that is needed for a given power decreases. Lower-voltage DC power requires more current than high-voltage AC power to generate the same amount of electricity.

Changeable AC current

Unlike DC current, AC current switches direction. If AC current enters the primary coil of a transformer *(near right)*, current fluctuations result in a changing magnetic field and a current in the secondary coil. Substituting DC current *(far right)* produces a steady current.

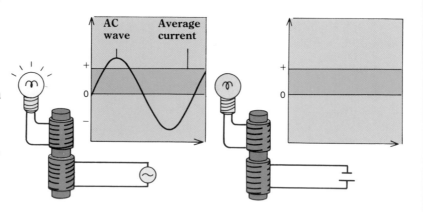

AC wave   Average current

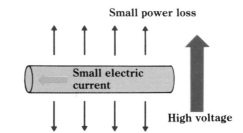

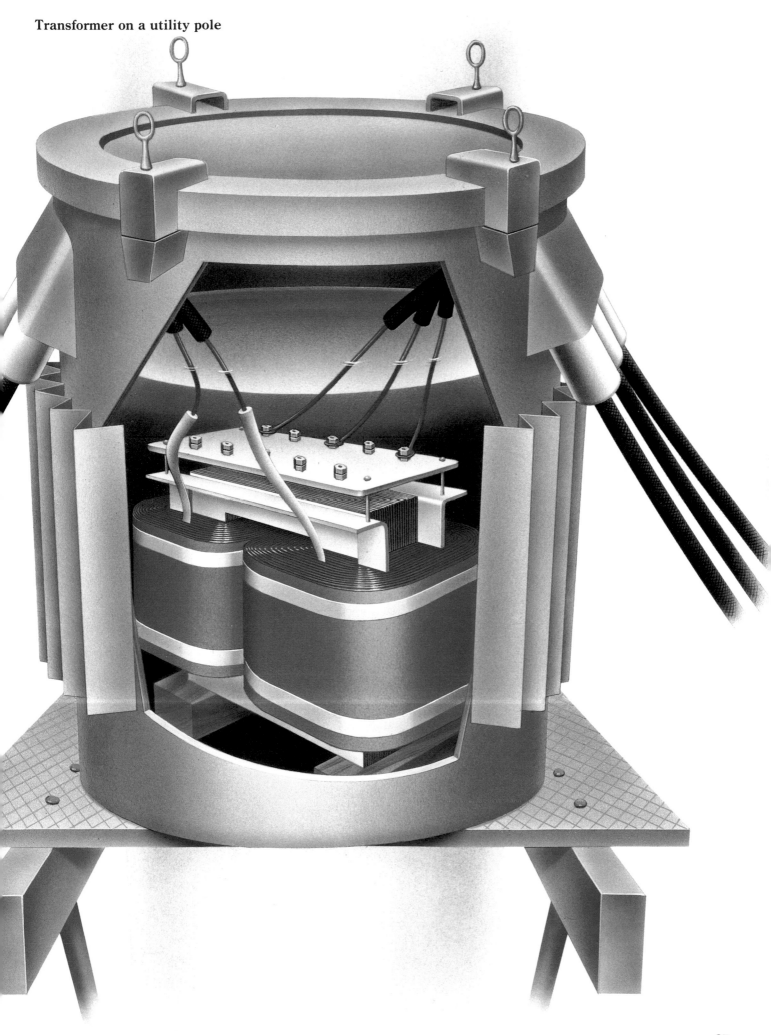

How Do Electromagnetic Waves Travel?

Any time an electric current varies its speed or course, it generates electromagnetic waves—fluctuations of electrical and magnetic force. One example is the changing current in a radio's transmitting antenna, which creates rings of expanding radio waves *(below)*.

The energy of an electromagnetic wave is related to its wavelength—the distance from one wave crest to the next. The shorter the wavelength, the more energetic the wave. In order of decreasing wavelength, electromagnetic waves include radio waves, infrared rays, visible light, ultraviolet light, x-rays, and gamma rays. Gamma rays are a mere one hundred-billionth of a meter or 3.3 hundred-billionths of a foot long, while radio waves can be a few miles long.

As electromagnetic waves spread outward at the speed of light, their electric and magnetic fields radiate at right angles to each other and to the direction of wave flow *(far right, top)*.

Wave mechanics

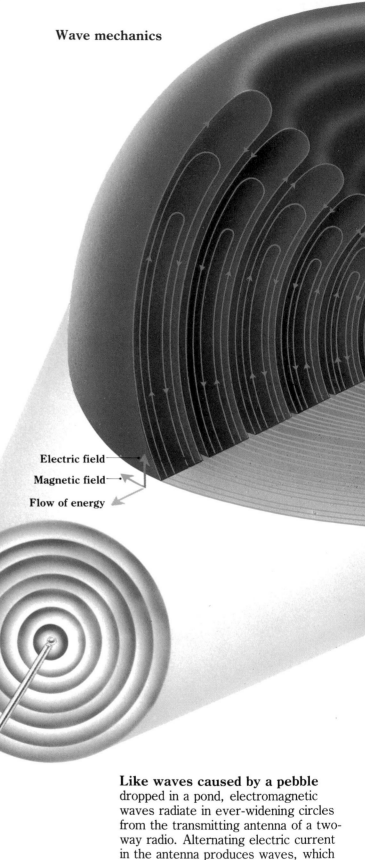

Electric field

Magnetic field

Flow of energy

Like waves caused by a pebble dropped in a pond, electromagnetic waves radiate in ever-widening circles from the transmitting antenna of a two-way radio. Alternating electric current in the antenna produces waves, which consist of electric and magnetic fields.

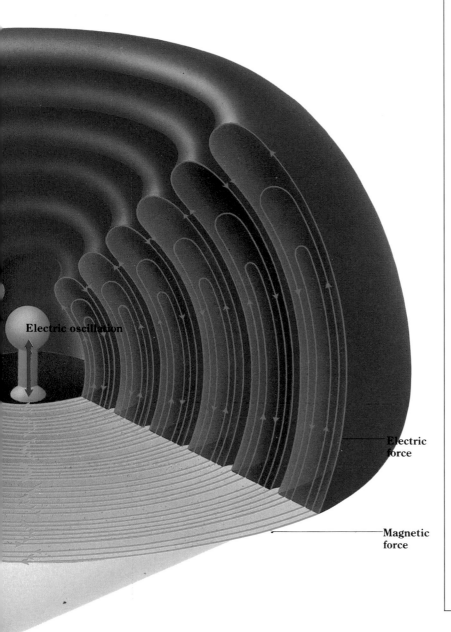

Electric oscillation

Electric force

Magnetic force

Charting electromagnetic waves

Electromagnetic waves travel in straight lines, with their electric and magnetic fields perpendicular to the energy flow.

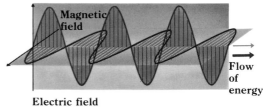

Magnetic field

Flow of energy

Electric field

When waves refract

Like light, all electromagnetic waves slow down and bend when they enter substances at anything other than a right angle.

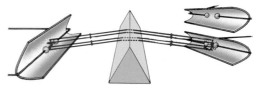

When waves reflect

If electromagnetic waves strike a metallic parabolic surface, they will focus at a single point.

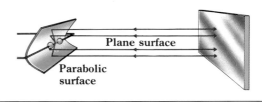

Plane surface

Parabolic surface

How waves grow

Electric field

Magnetic field

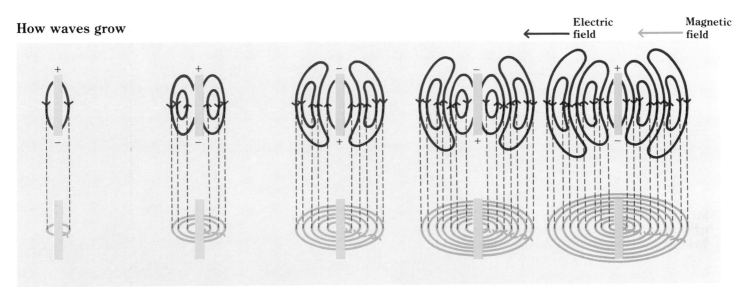

The complex wave pattern that emanates from a transmitting antenna builds from a single fluctuation of current. When the current flows up the antenna, the electric field *(red)* moves from top to bottom and the magnetic field *(green)* rotates counterclockwise. As the current reverses direction, the electric and magnetic fields follow suit.

89

What Other Energy Comes from Atoms?

The current that powers machinery and generates electromagnetism is only one of the energy forms resulting from an atom's electrical properties. Another is radioactivity—the energy released when an atom's nucleus breaks down.

Atoms consist of negatively charged electrons, positively charged protons, and neutral particles called neutrons. Invisible forces of unimaginable strength bind an atom's protons and neutrons together in the nucleus. The nuclei of nearly all atoms disintegrate over time, unleashing some of this energy in the form of high-energy alpha and beta particles and gamma rays.

Though it cannot be seen, such radiation can be detected with electronic devices. The Geiger counter, perhaps the best-known radiation detector, translates the energy from radiation into measurable electronic signals.

Detecting radiation

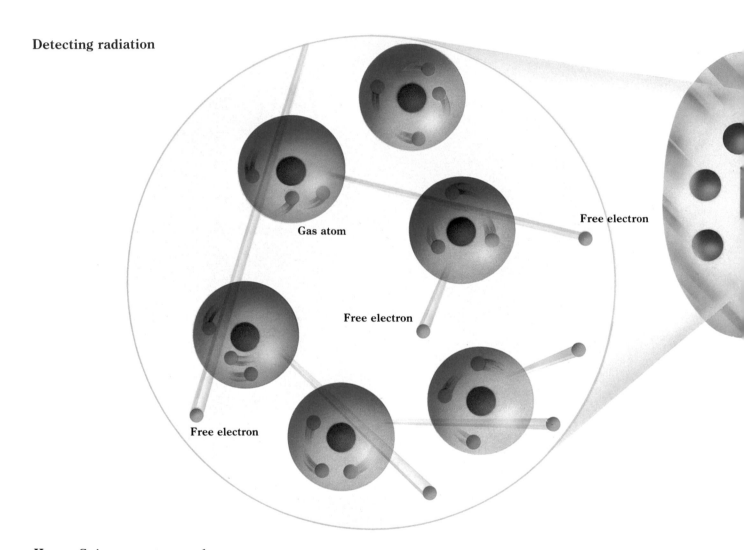

Gas atom

Free electron

Free electron

Free electron

How a Geiger counter works

When a radioactive particle collides with a gas atom, it liberates an electron from the gas atom. This electron travels toward the center electrode's positive voltage but may strike another atom en route. A succession of collisions sets off an electron avalanche that registers as an electric pulse on the center electrode.

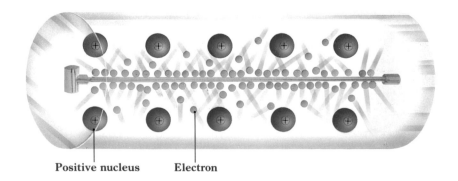

Positive nucleus   Electron

Geiger counter basics

The counter's metal tube doubles as a gas cylinder and negative electrode. In its center is a positive electrode. Radiation enters the counter's mica window and bombards gas atoms, causing an electron storm between the electrodes.

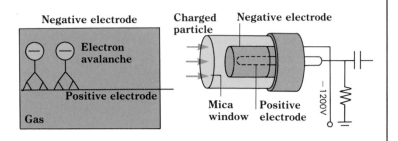

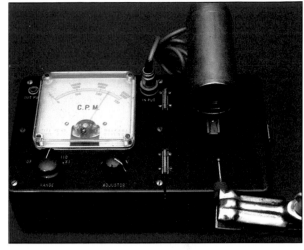

Geiger counter and pulse meter

Radiation particle — — Gas atom

Negative electrode

Positive electrode

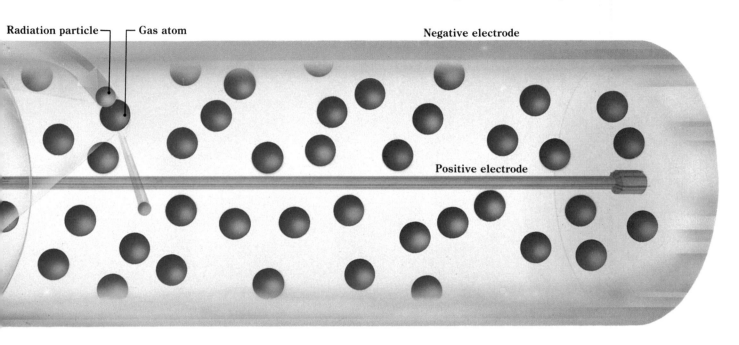

Alpha, beta, and gamma decay

In alpha and beta decay, the elements become new substances. In gamma decay, only the arrangement of nuclear protons and neutrons changes. Shown here at top right, a neodymium-144 nucleus undergoes alpha decay, releasing an alpha particle to become a cerium-140 nucleus. At center, beta decay turns lithium 8 into beryllium 8 by converting a lithium neutron into a proton and emitting a beta particle and a neutral particle known as a neutrino. In the bottom example of gamma decay, excess nuclear energy in a sodium-24 atom escapes as a gamma ray, but the atom is otherwise unchanged.

Proton   Neutron   Beta particle

Alpha particle

Alpha decay

Neodymium-144 nucleus

Cerium-140 nucleus

Beta decay

Beta particle

Lithium-8 nucleus

Neutrino

Beryllium 8

Gamma decay

Gamma ray

Sodium-24 nucleus

Sodium-24 nucleus

What Is Superconductivity?

Among the twentieth century's most exciting discoveries is that of superconductivity. When superchilled, some substances have the ability to conduct electricity without resistance and that makes them superconductors.

In 1911, when Dutch physicist Heike Kamerlingh Onnes used helium to cool a mercury wire to 4° K., or −453° F., he was amazed to find that current passed through the wire without resistance. Today, scientists can create substances that exhibit these superconducting properties at higher temperatures, up to 100° K., or −280° F. The revolutionary substances led to some exciting concepts—among them superconducting magnetic energy storage and generators in power systems, electromagnetically powered launch vehicles, and superconducting trains and boats—which combine superconductors' surprising conductivity with their strange magnetic properties. Placed in a magnetic field, superconductors generate their own magnetic field of like polarity, causing magnetized objects to hover.

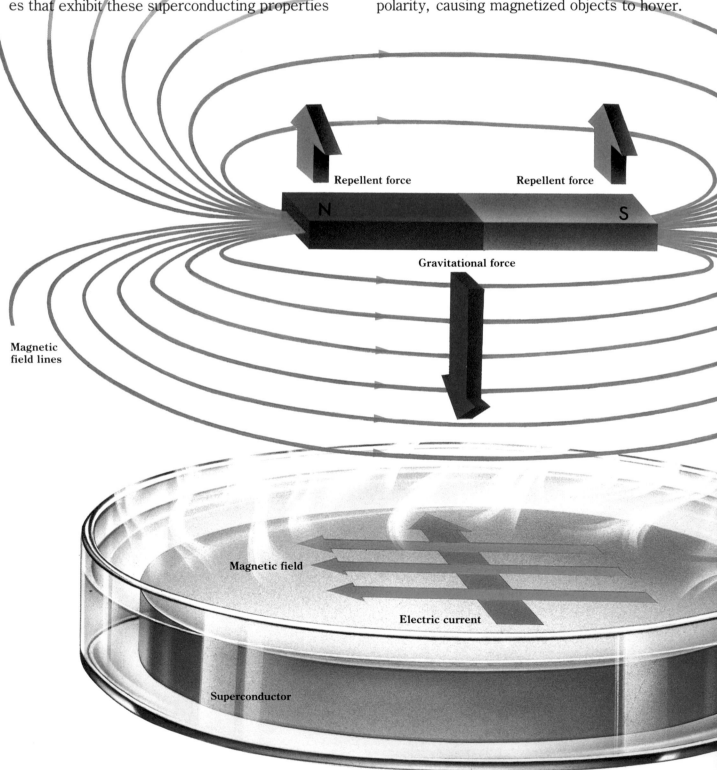

Repellent force   Repellent force

N   S

Gravitational force

Magnetic field lines

Magnetic field

Electric current

Superconductor

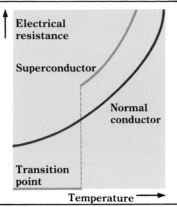

As the temperature is reduced, electrical resistance diminishes in normal conductors *(purple)*, while superconductors *(blue)* reach a so-called transition point temperature at which their electrical resistance suddenly becomes zero.

Conventional conductors

Not only do normal conductors channel current less efficiently than superconductors *(below)*, but they also exhibit none of the superconductors' magical repellent properties, as shown in the illustration at far left.

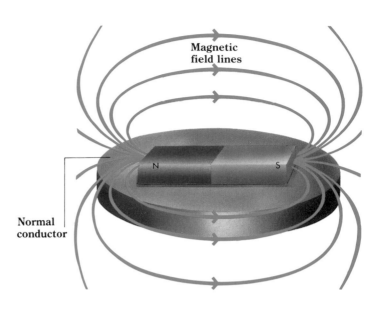

The Meissner effect

A superconductor's magnetic properties are unlike those of a ferromagnetic conductor such as iron. Placed in a magnetic field, ferromagnetic materials become attracted to magnets. Superconductors, in what is called the Meissner effect, are repelled by magnets.

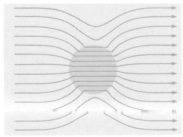
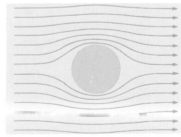

Ferromagnetic conductor   Superconductor

Superconducting levitation

A magnet placed above a helium-cooled superconductor induces an electric current and an electromagnetic field that repulse the magnet's magnetic force, causing the magnet to float.

— Liquid helium

A superconducting train

One futuristic train design from Japan proposes superconducting magnets for propulsion. Superconductors in the train's undercarriage are repelled by the track's magnetic field, causing the train to levitate. Until the train is moving fast enough to lift off, it rolls on wheels.

As the superconductors move faster and faster over the magnetic field in the track, the magnetic force increases, raising the train 4 inches above the track.

6

Generating Electricity

In 1831, when English physicist Michael Faraday was conducting experiments with electricity, he hooked the two leads of a current-measuring device to a copper disk. He attached one electrode to the center of the disk, the other to the edge, and spun the disk between the poles of a powerful magnet. As the disk twirled, electricity flowed through the circuit, and as the disk spun faster, the current increased. With this playful experimentation, Faraday, who became one of England's most famous scientists, had invented the dynamo, the first electrical generator.

Modern electrical generators, from portable gasoline-powered models to huge hydroelectric generating stations, are more complex and produce far more current than Faraday's dynamo, but all of these generators operate on the same principle: When a magnet moves past a coil of wire, a current flows through the wire. This phenomenon is known as electromagnetic induction. Dutch physicist Hans Christian Ørsted had discovered the connection between electrical and magnetic forces in 1819, when he observed that a moving electric current produces a magnetic field. Faraday, trying to understand this effect, created his hand-powered dynamo. Today, scientists harness the energy of moving water, sunlight, atoms, fossil fuels, hot underground rocks, and wind to move magnets past coils of wire, generating the electricity that makes modern society possible.

A faint blue glow emanates from the water covering a nuclear reactor core, the heart of a nuclear-powered generator. The splitting of atoms is just one of many ways in which power is produced to run electric generators.

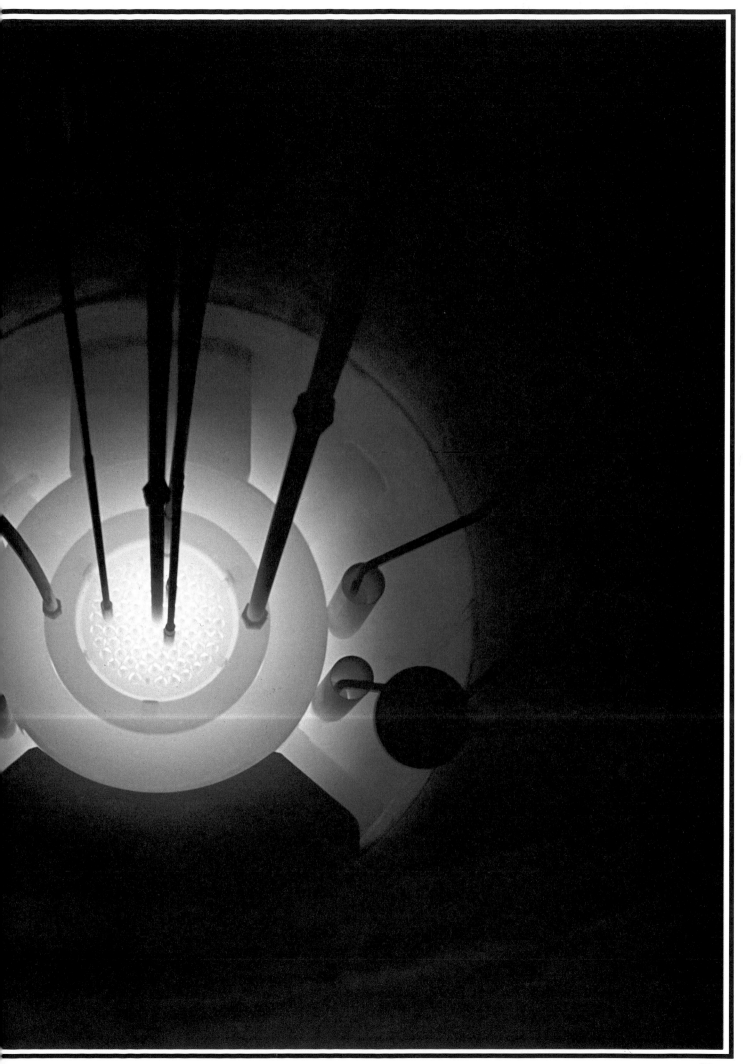

How Does an AC Generator Work?

A generator converts mechanical energy into electrical energy by means of a wire coil that is rotated in a magnetic field. An electric current is also produced when the force lines of a magnet pass through a wire coil *(right)*. The electrons *(blue)* flow toward the magnet's positive pole, and the current moves from the positive pole to the negative pole. As long as the magnetic field moves through the coil, or conductor, current is induced in the conductor. The same principle applies when a wire coil passes near a magnet *(far right)* and the coil moves through the magnetic field. The induced current flows in such a way that it repels the magnet when the magnet comes close to the coil, and it attracts the magnet when the magnet moves away. Each time the magnet changes direction relative to the coil, the current changes direction, or alternates, as well. As long as a device mechanically rotates the conductor, or the magnetic field, the generator will continue to produce a flow of alternating current (AC).

Induced current

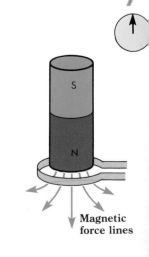

Changing current direction

When a magnet is moved through a wire coil *(below)*, it induces an electric current to flow in the coil. This current causes the needle on the galvanometer *(pages 76-77)* to swing away from the zero position. When the magnet is pulled back through the coil, the current changes directions, or alternates, and the galvanometer needle swings to the opposite side of the zero position.

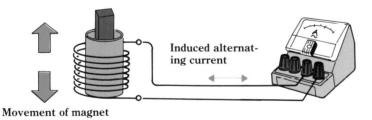

Induced alternating current

Movement of magnet

Alternating current

A magnet will not induce a current until its force lines cross the wire coil. Moving a magnet's pole into a coil induces a current to flow in the wire loop. When the magnet stops moving, the current *(blue arrows)* stops flowing *(middle diagram)*. Pulling the magnet away from the coil induces a current flowing in the opposite direction.

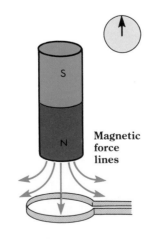

Magnetic force lines

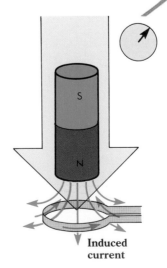

Induced current

Magnetic force lines

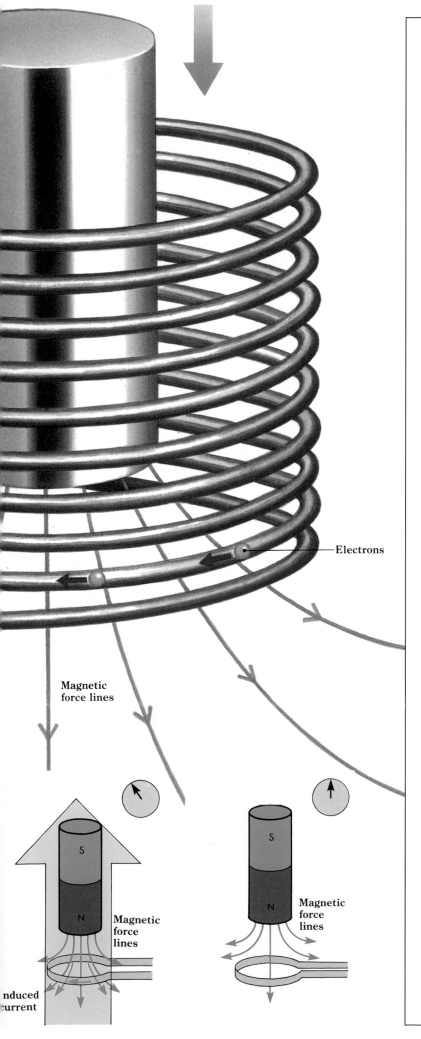

Electrons

Magnetic force lines

Magnetic force lines

Magnetic force lines

Induced current

A basic AC generator

In a simple AC generator, a wire loop spins between the poles of a stationary magnet. Each end of the loop connects to a slip ring that rubs against a conducting carbon brush *(below)*. The induced current flows to the inner slip ring as its half of the loop passes the north pole, but the current flows toward the outer ring as the other half of the loop spins past the north pole.

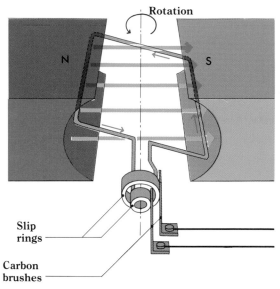

Rotation

N   S

Slip rings

Carbon brushes

Three-phase AC generator

An economical way of producing strong alternating current is to use one magnet spinning past several coils. In the common three-phase generator *(below)*, three coils sit equally spaced around the magnet. Each coil produces an alternating current as the magnet passes *(bottom)*.

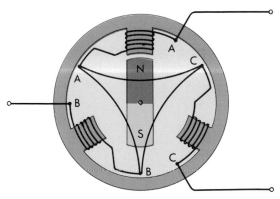

Three-phase AC generator

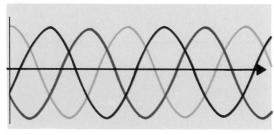

Outputs from three coils

97

How Does Water Provide Electricity?

Water has long provided power to meet human needs, and today, hydroelectric generators produce about 20 percent of the world's electricity. Water from behind a dam falls past giant turbine blades, spinning them at speeds of 125 to 750 revolutions per minute. The whirling blades provide the mechanical power that turns the huge magnet inside an AC generator. How much power is produced depends on the water's "head"— how far the water falls before reaching the turbine. Engineers have developed turbines to harness the power from a head as low as 20 feet and as high as 5,800 feet.

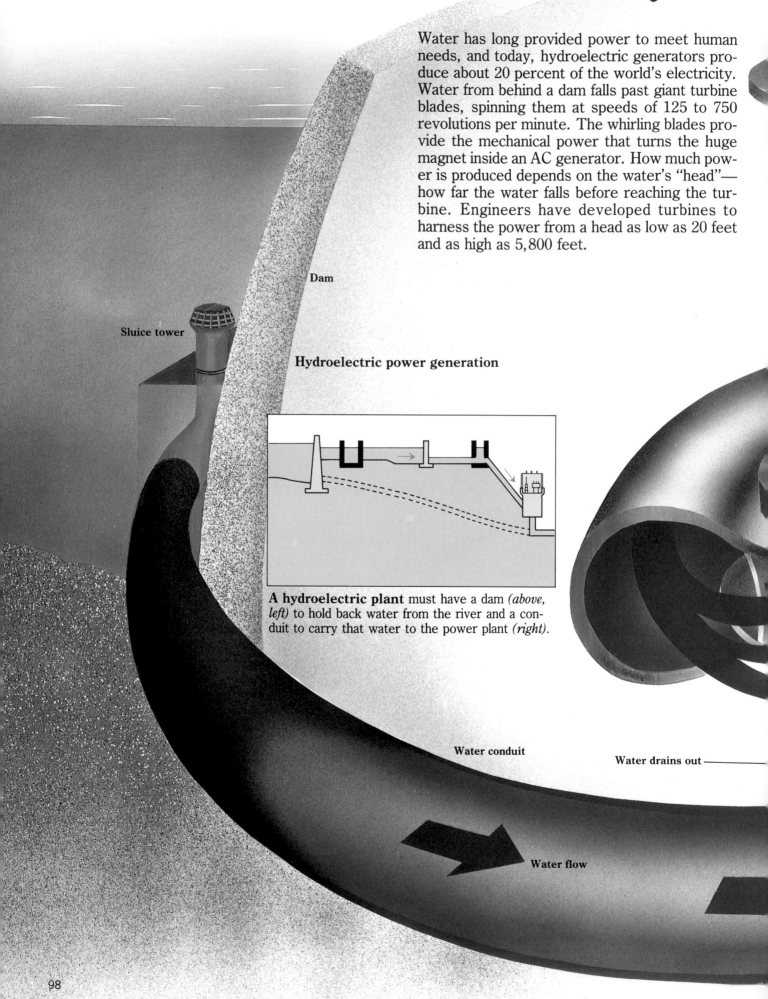

Dam

Sluice tower

Hydroelectric power generation

A hydroelectric plant must have a dam *(above, left)* to hold back water from the river and a conduit to carry that water to the power plant *(right)*.

Water conduit

Water drains out ─

Water flow

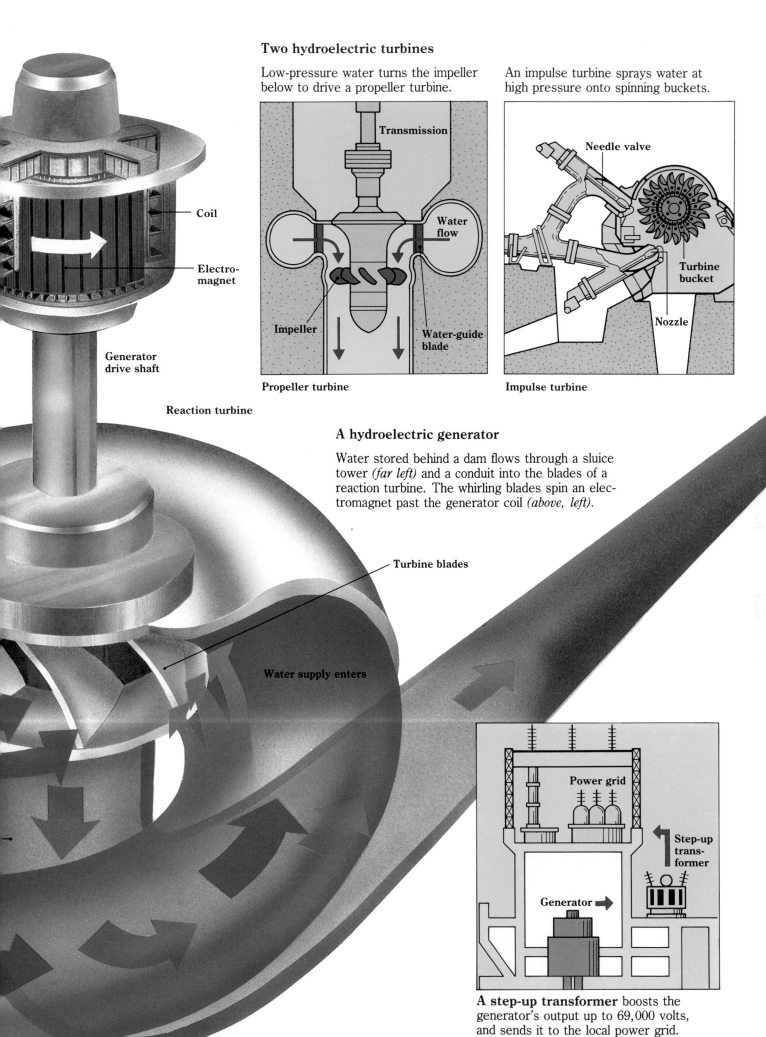

Two hydroelectric turbines

Low-pressure water turns the impeller below to drive a propeller turbine.

An impulse turbine sprays water at high pressure onto spinning buckets.

Coil

Electro-magnet

Generator drive shaft

Reaction turbine

Transmission

Water flow

Impeller

Water-guide blade

Propeller turbine

Needle valve

Turbine bucket

Nozzle

Impulse turbine

A hydroelectric generator

Water stored behind a dam flows through a sluice tower *(far left)* and a conduit into the blades of a reaction turbine. The whirling blades spin an electromagnet past the generator coil *(above, left)*.

Turbine blades

Water supply enters

Power grid

Step-up transformer

Generator

A step-up transformer boosts the generator's output up to 69,000 volts, and sends it to the local power grid.

How Do Power Plants Use Fossil Fuels?

A thermoelectric power plant uses energy released from the burning of fossil fuels—coal, oil, and natural gas—to convert water into high-pressure steam. The steam, at a pressure of about 3,500 pounds per square inch and a temperature of 524° C., or 1,000° F., drives a turbine. The turbine spins a huge magnet inside a generator, producing electricity.

Modern thermoelectric plants capture about 40 percent of the energy released from burning fuels and convert it into electricity; the rest of the energy is lost as heat. Many power plants in Europe use the waste heat to warm nearby homes and businesses. Producing both usable heat and electricity increases the energy efficiency to 80 percent.

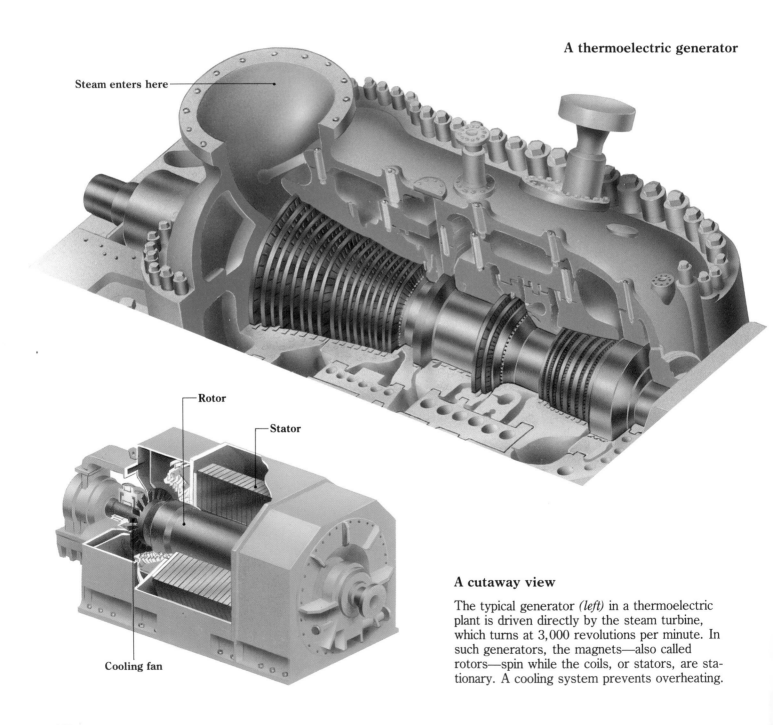

A thermoelectric generator

Steam enters here

Rotor

Stator

Cooling fan

A cutaway view

The typical generator *(left)* in a thermoelectric plant is driven directly by the steam turbine, which turns at 3,000 revolutions per minute. In such generators, the magnets—also called rotors—spin while the coils, or stators, are stationary. A cooling system prevents overheating.

Impeller blades are visible in this steam turbine.

A typical steam turbine *(left)* contains two sets of blades. High-pressure steam, fresh from the boiler, enters the turbine chamber and spins the first set of blades. The steam is reheated and circulated back to the turbine chamber to drive a second set of blades that operate at lower steam pressure.

An oil, coal, or gas boiler

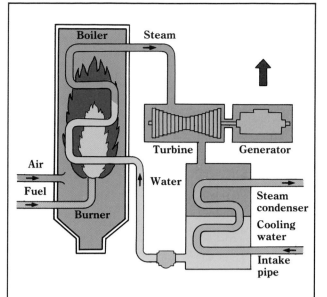

Generating power with steam

In a thermoelectric plant, fuel burns in a boiler, producing an intensely hot flame. Pipes carry water through the flame, and the heat turns the water to high-pressure steam. The steam drives a turbine, providing the mechanical energy that a generator converts to electricity. After leaving the turbine, the steam travels to a condenser, where it circulates over pipes carrying cold water and is turned back into water.

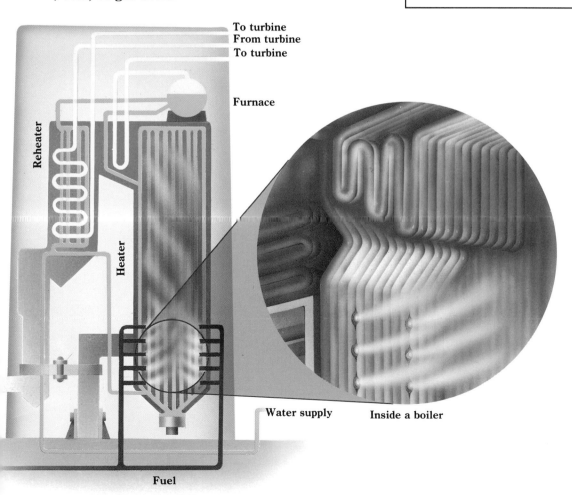

Inside a boiler

Inside a boiler

A boiler is filled with water-carrying pipes folded upon themselves many times over. This configuration maximizes the amount of heat transferred to the water and thus produces the most steam.

What Is Geothermal Generation?

Ten miles beneath Earth's surface, an almost limitless source of energy waits to be mined. It's not oil, coal, or natural gas, but the energy from the rocky, hot interior of 420° C., or 800° F., or more. This intense heat, known as geothermal energy, turns underground water into the steam that erupts from geysers such as Old Faithful in Yellowstone National Park. It also powers steam-turbine electrical generators built over geysers in California, New Zealand, and Italy.

Getting steam from the Earth

Water pumped into a geothermal well returns to the surface as high-pressure steam and super-heated water *(below)*. This mixture passes into a cyclone separator, a device that traps the water and lets the steam flow to the turbine. The steam spins the turbine's impellers, driving the generator and producing electricity. The water can also be used to provide heat for homes and businesses before it is returned to the ground.

These natural pockets of steam, within a mile of the surface, are too rare to provide large amounts of natural geothermal energy world-wide. But holes drilled 10 miles deep into the ground can reach geothermal energy and create steam anywhere a power plant is needed.

There are two ways to drill for geothermal energy, both using holes bored 50,000 feet deep or more. One method uses a single hole about 2 feet in diameter. Cold water poured down the hole is heated by the surrounding rocks and returns as steam through an insulated inner pipe. The other method uses several narrower holes. Water pumped down one hole percolates through the hot rocks and returns to the surface as steam through insulated pipes in "riser" holes.

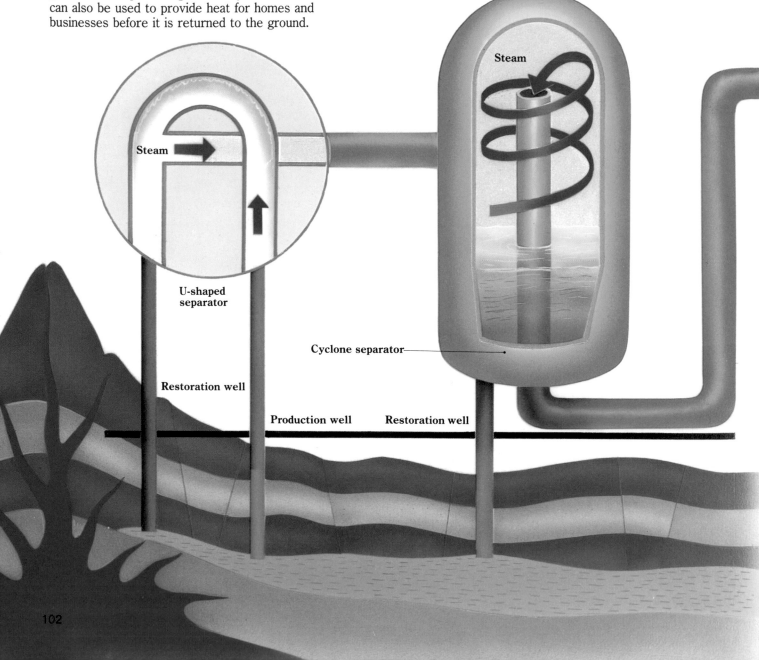

Steam

Steam

U-shaped separator

Cyclone separator

Restoration well

Production well   Restoration well

Two-way generation

A plant like this produces electricity with hot geothermal water to vaporize a chemical compound *(purple)* that has a boiling point far below that of water. The pressure of the chemical steam drives a turbine.

The steam-water cycle

This plant uses steam *(lilac)* that is separated from the hot water *(pink)* at the production well, then used to drive the turbine. The water is restored to the ground. The steam is later cooled and recirculated as water.

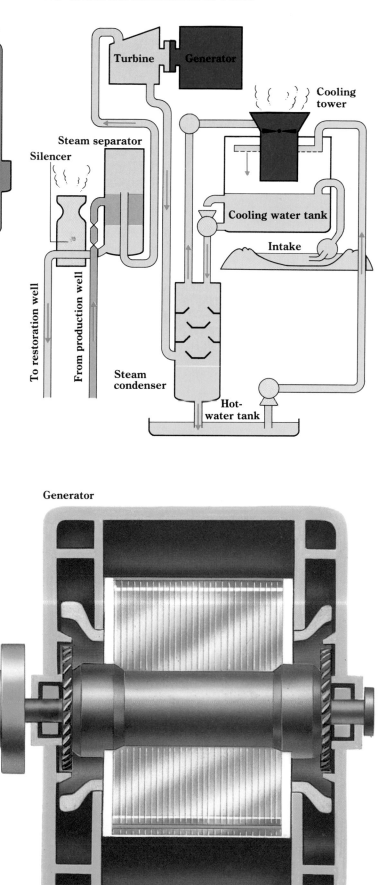

Generator

Turbine

Air-cooled condenser

Steam separator

Cooling tower

Steam generator

Flash heater

Restoration well

Production well

Turbine

Generator

Cooling tower

Steam separator

Silencer

Cooling water tank

Intake

To restoration well

From production well

Steam condenser

Hot-water tank

Steam turbine

Generator

How Is Wind Used as a Power Source?

In many parts of the world, including California and the midwestern United States, brisk winds are common enough to serve as an inexpensive and reliable source of nonpolluting energy for generating electricity. Windmills come in a variety of shapes and sizes, each designed for a particular task and setting. For example, the Darrieus windmill, which has a rotor that resembles an eggbeater, works most efficiently at high wind speeds. The kind of windmill with four or eight blades that is used on a farm is best suited for generating small amounts of direct current to run water pumps in areas with mild winds.

The basic windmill consists of one or more blades, a mechanism to keep the blades rotating at a constant speed in the face of changing winds,

and a generator. A widely used kind of windmill *(below)* has two blades and looks like an airplane propeller mounted on a tall pole. But unlike an airplane propeller, these windmill blades are able to change shape in response to varying winds. They are built this way because windmills that are part of a utility grid need to operate at near-constant speeds to keep their electrical output steady. Gears and wind brakes also help keep the windmill operating at peak efficiency.

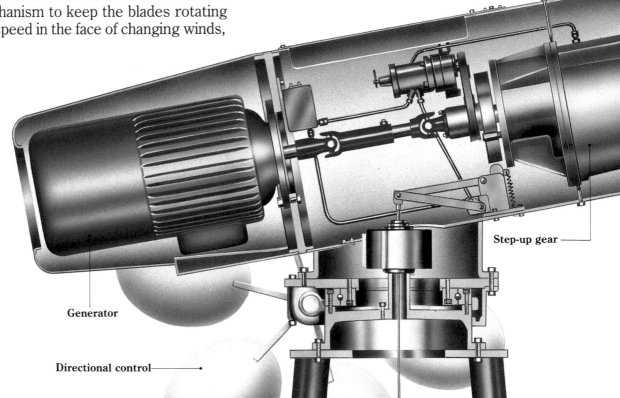

Generator

Step-up gear

Directional control

● **The Darrieus windmill**

The Darrieus rotor is equipped with two curved, vertical blades that spin around a power shaft. A rounded leading edge and sharp trailing edge reduce friction. The Darrieus rotor works best in strong winds.

Blade in cross section

Wind

This wind farm in northern California has dozens of windmills that convert the area's strong winds into electricity. Each windmill is carefully placed so that it will not prevent the full force of the wind from reaching any of the others.

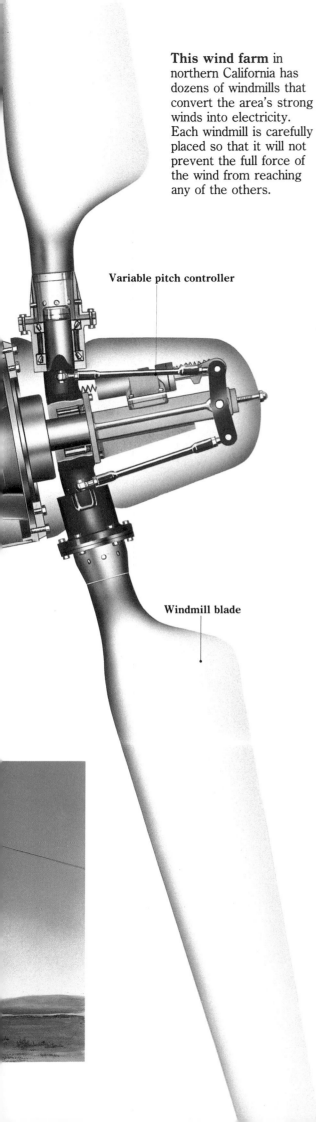

Variable pitch controller

Windmill blade

Adjusting to changing winds

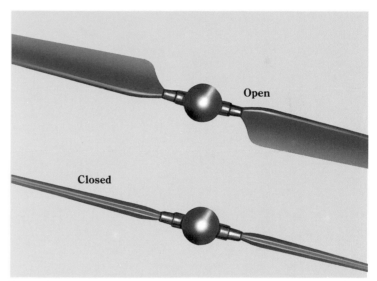

Open

Closed

In weak winds, the windmill blades above open *(top)* to catch as much of the wind energy as possible. When the wind increases, the blades close *(bottom)*, so as not to turn too fast.

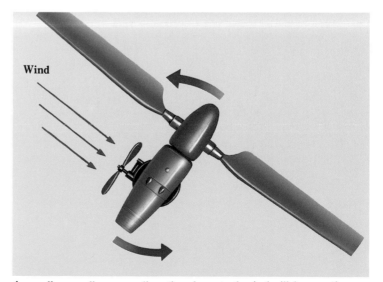

Wind

A small propeller on a directional control windmill keeps the main propeller facing into the wind. This helps the windmill capture the wind's energy most efficiently.

How Is the Ocean's Power Harnessed?

The ocean can be tapped for three different forms of energy—tidal, wave, and thermal power. To capture the energy in tides, a dike is built across an estuary *(below)*. Tunnels running through the dike house turbines and generators. When the tide comes in, the water level is higher on the ocean side of the dike. This imbalance forces water to flow through the tunnel to the low water side, spinning the turbine as it goes. At low tide, the water is higher in the estuary than on the ocean side. The water flows back through the tunnel, producing more electricity.

Wave power also uses the ebb and flow of wa-

ter to spin a turbine set inside a bottomless float. When a wave swells beneath the float, it forces air past the turbine blades twice—once when the water is high and again when the water drops.

Ocean thermal power generation uses the sharp difference in temperature between the ocean's surface and its depths to evaporate and condense a liquid that will vaporize at a low temperature. The vapor drives a turbine.

■ **Tidal power generating station**

Dike

● **Harnessing the tides**

The turbine in a tidal power generating station produces electricity whether the tide is coming in *(below, left)* or going out *(below, right)*.

General

Turbine propeller

Water pressure

Reservoir

← **High tide**

→ **Low tide**

Capturing the power of waves

Wave water falling *(right)* under the bell of a floating wave-power generator pulls air in past twin turbine blades. Cresting water *(far right)* expels air, spinning the turbines the other way. The ship is a platform for such generators.

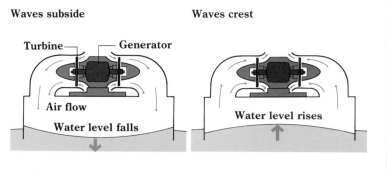

Waves subside

Waves crest

Turbine — — Generator

Air flow

Water level falls

Water level rises

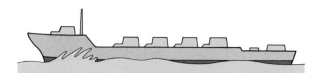

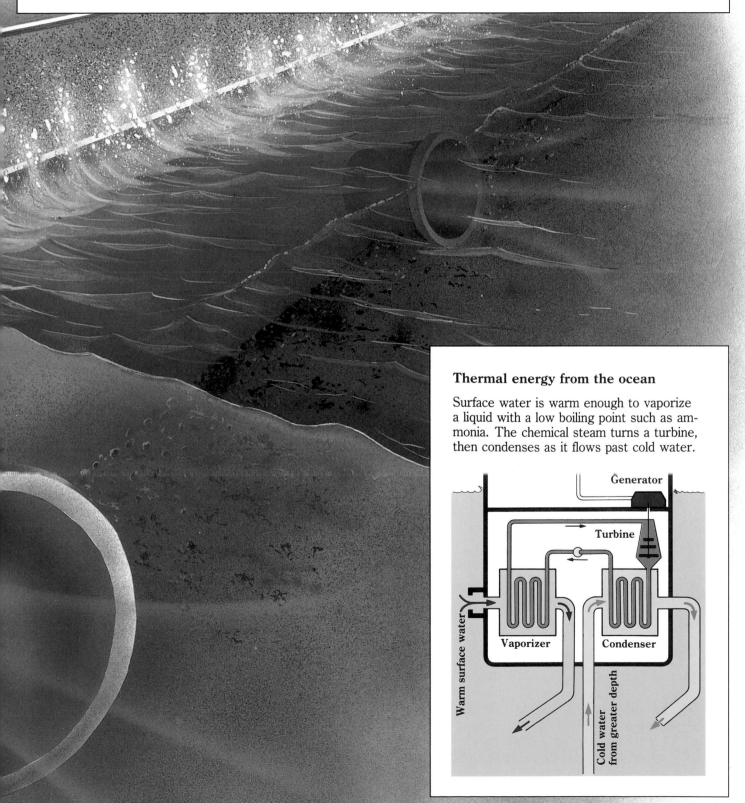

Thermal energy from the ocean

Surface water is warm enough to vaporize a liquid with a low boiling point such as ammonia. The chemical steam turns a turbine, then condenses as it flows past cold water.

Generator

Turbine

Warm surface water

Vaporizer

Condenser

Cold water from greater depth

How Does a Nuclear Reactor Work?

The radioactive core of a nuclear-powered reactor—the most concentrated form of energy used today—sits in a steel tank with 6-inch-thick walls. The core contains uranium 235 in the form of ½-inch pellets stacked inside dozens of 10-foot-long stainless steel tubes. The atoms of uranium 235 undergo fission—that is, they split apart—and every atom that splits releases tremendous amounts of energy. The fission of 1 gram, or 0.035 ounce, of uranium 235 releases as much energy as the burning of more than 500 gallons of oil. Water moving through the core heats a second supply of water to make steam, which turns a turbine.

Besides producing energy, fissioning uranium 235 atoms release neutrons, one of two main types of particles in the atomic nucleus. The neutrons strike other uranium 235 atoms, splitting them and releasing still more neutrons to produce a chain reaction, a continuous energy source. To control this chain reaction, rods of boron or cadmium—materials that absorb neutrons—are lowered into the core.

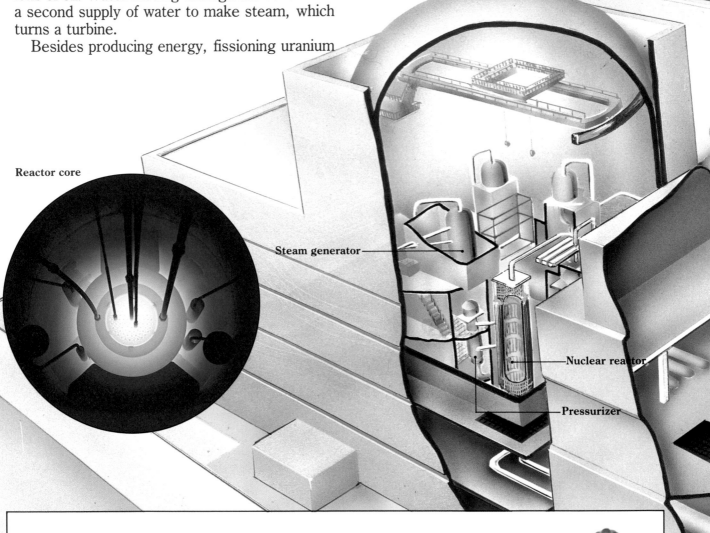

Reactor core

Steam generator

Nuclear reactor

Pressurizer

Chain reaction of uranium 235

An atom of uranium 235 becomes unstable and splits into two smaller atoms when struck by a neutron. This is nuclear fission. When uranium 235 splits, it releases two or three neutrons that can strike other atoms of uranium 235, starting a self-perpetuating chain reaction.

Uranium 235

Uranium 235

Uranium 235

Uranium 235

● Proton

● Neutron

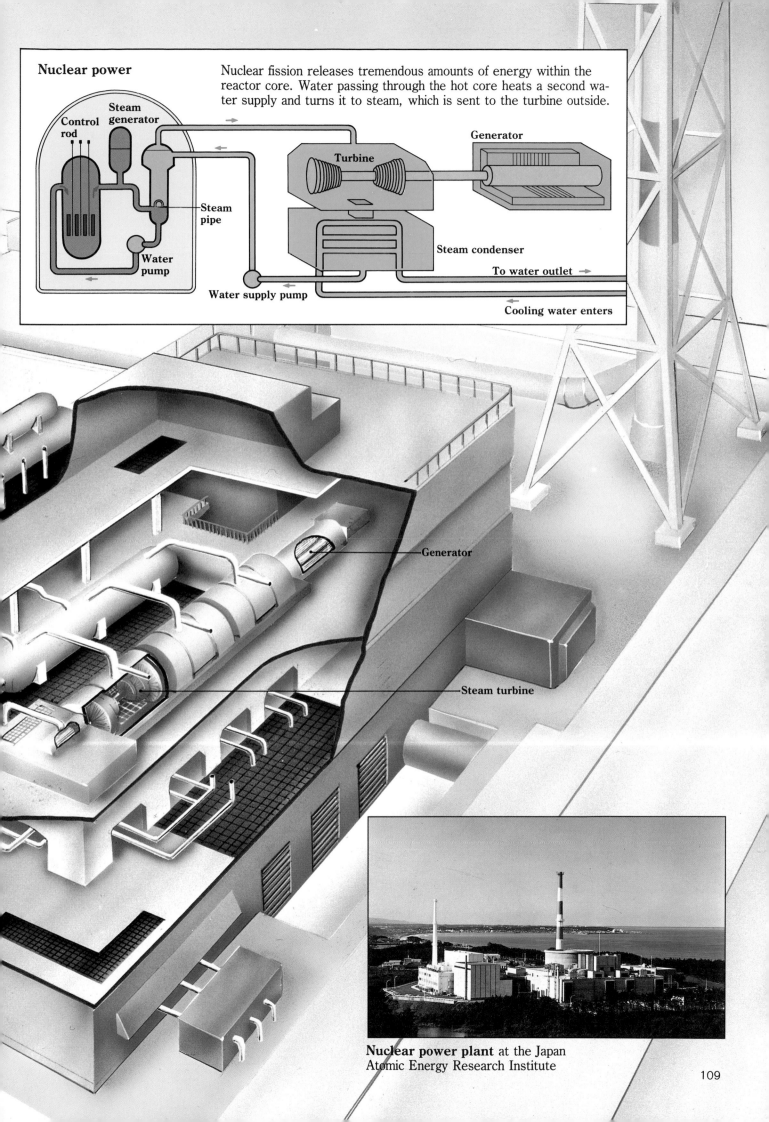

Nuclear power

Nuclear fission releases tremendous amounts of energy within the reactor core. Water passing through the hot core heats a second water supply and turns it to steam, which is sent to the turbine outside.

Control rod

Steam generator

Generator

Turbine

Steam pipe

Steam condenser

Water pump

To water outlet

Water supply pump

Cooling water enters

Generator

Steam turbine

Nuclear power plant at the Japan Atomic Energy Research Institute

How Is Solar Power Generated?

Sunlight, the energy source that makes all life possible, may someday furnish much of the electricity on which modern society runs. Sunlight can be used indirectly to power a turbine. A set of mirrors focuses the sun's energy onto a heat exchanger, which vaporizes water or some other liquid, producing steam to drive a conventional turbine and generator. Silicon solar cells, however, generate electricity directly from sunlight.

A typical solar cell consists of six layers. The base doubles as the cell's negative pole; a reflec-

tive layer keeps light within the working part of the cell, boosting the cell's electrical output. Two layers of treated silicon—N-type and P-type—form the heart of the solar cell. N-type silicon has free negative charges and P-type silicon has unbound positive charges. In darkness, the charges gather at the junction between layers; when sunlight hits the cell, they move apart. This movement creates a direct current when the cell is part of a circuit. A clear film protects the silicon, and a metal positive pole completes the cell.

The structure of a solar cell

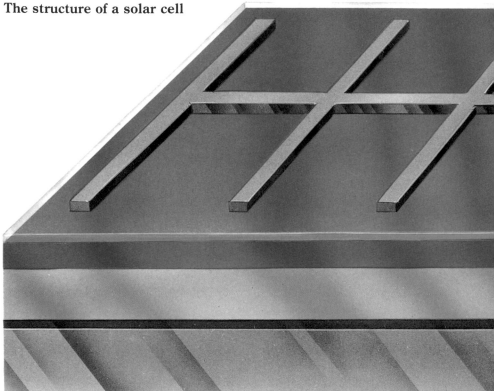

The solar battery in a calculator can run on ordinary room lights.

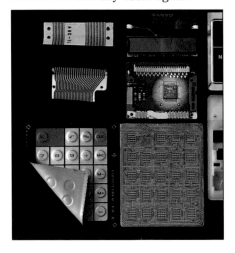

How a solar cell works

Sunlight striking a solar cell separates the positive and negative charges that accumulate at the junction between slabs of P-type and N-type silicon. The separation creates a voltage that generates a current when the cell is part of a complete circuit.

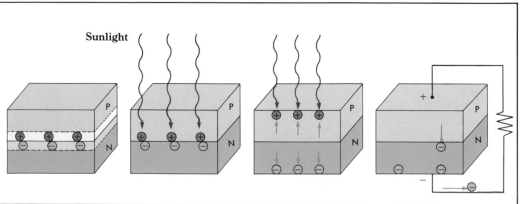

A solar cell array

Solar cells *(below)* produce direct current, which can be converted to alternating current at a power plant. Excess solar-generated electricity can be stored in batteries for later use.

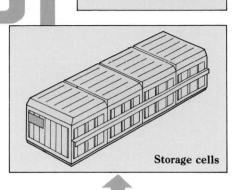

Power plant

Transformer

House

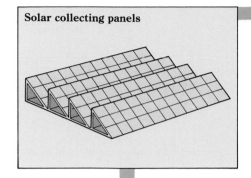

Solar collecting panels

Storage cells

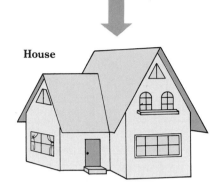

Solar batteries in space

Solar cells have been the prime energy source for most space satellites. These cells *(right)* differ from those used on Earth *(left)*. While earth-bound solar cells need protection from rain and dirt, those that function in space must resist high-energy radiation.

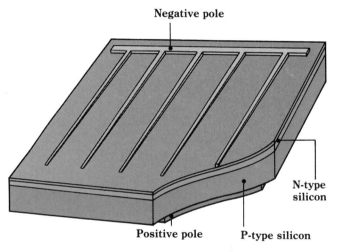

Negative pole

N-type silicon

Positive pole   **P-type silicon**

- Negative pole (base)
- Reflecting layer
- N-type silicon
- P-type silicon
- Clear conducting film
- Positive pole

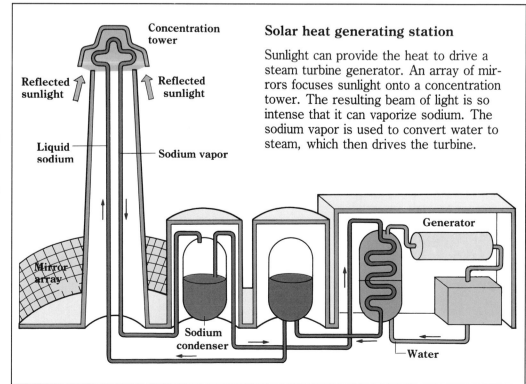

Concentration tower

Solar heat generating station

Sunlight can provide the heat to drive a steam turbine generator. An array of mirrors focuses sunlight onto a concentration tower. The resulting beam of light is so intense that it can vaporize sodium. The sodium vapor is used to convert water to steam, which then drives the turbine.

Reflected sunlight

Reflected sunlight

Liquid sodium

Sodium vapor

Mirror array

Generator

Sodium condenser

Water

7
The Mysteries of Light

Almost everything scientists know about the universe comes from observing and analyzing light. Yet little was known about light itself until fairly recently. In the seventeenth century, two compelling theories about the nature of light emerged. The corpuscular theory, championed by Sir Isaac Newton, held that light consisted of tiny particles called corpuscles. Another theory proposed that light was a wave, moving through space in much the same way that ripples move across a pond. Although nearly every discovery about light's behavior during the next 200 years seemed to support the wave theory and discredit the corpuscular theory, the advent of quantum physics in the twentieth century reconciled the two theories: Depending on how it is measured and observed, light may assume the characteristics of either a particle or a wave.

Light has five distinct properties: propagation, reflection, refraction, diffraction, and interference. Propagation refers to the transmission of light in straight lines. Reflection causes light to bounce off polished surfaces such as mirrors. Light refracts, or bends, when it travels from one substance to another, for example from air through a glass lens. Light waves also will bend around an obstacle's edges, a phenomenon known as diffraction. In interference, intersecting light waves alter each other as they meet. Taken together, these properties explain the workings of devices as varied as magnifying glasses, lasers, and holograms.

The dazzling brilliance of lasers illustrates one of the many ways scientists can control light. Lasers amplify a single wavelength of light to produce a powerful, tightly focused beam that is useful in medicine, industry, and communications.

How Do Curved Surfaces Affect Light?

Light reflects differently off shiny surfaces depending on their curvature. The bowl of a spoon, for instance, gives upside-down reflections, while the spoon's back reflects images right side up. The determining factor in the reflection's position is the shape of the reflector. Concave surfaces such as the inner surface of a hollow sphere or the spoon's bowl often produce inverted images. Convex surfaces such as the exterior of a sphere or the back of the spoon produce reflections right side up.

Concave mirrors reflect light rays inward, directing them to a single spot called the focal point. The rays cross at the place where the image forms. If the object being reflected by a concave mirror lies closer to the mirror than does

the focal point, the resulting image will be right side up. If the object lies beyond the focal point, its reflection will be inverted. Reflections from a convex surface, however, are always right side up because such surfaces cause reflected light rays to diverge rather than converge. As a result, the reflected rays never cross each other to produce an inverted image.

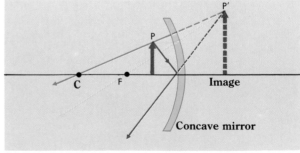

Key:

P = Object

P' = Image

C = Center of sphere

F = Focal point

1

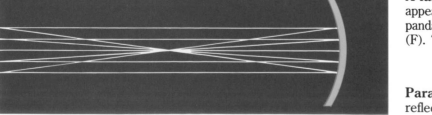

A larger-than-life image (P') of the panda *(above)* appears in a spherical, concave mirror when the panda (P) is between the mirror and the focal point (F). The image forms where reflected rays cross.

Parallel rays converge at the focal point as they reflect off the concave surface of a spherical mirror.

3

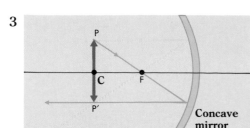

The reflection is still inverted but looks life-size when the panda sits at the center of the spherical mirror.

2

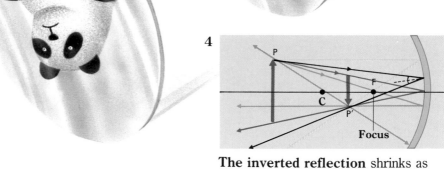

3

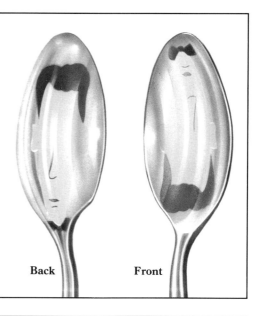

4

4

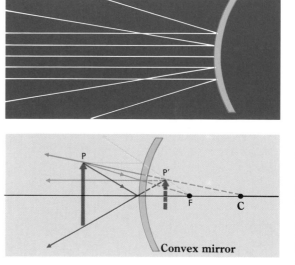

The inverted reflection shrinks as the panda moves away from the center of the mirror.

2

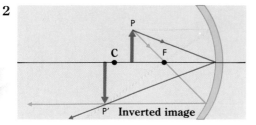

An upside-down but still larger-than-life image appears when the panda sits between the focal point and the center of the sphere.

Faces in a spoon

The inner and outer surfaces of a spoon act like the concave and convex surfaces of a spherical mirror. Because the focal point of the spoon's bowl is so close to the spoon, the reflected face will always be upside down. The convex back of the spoon always yields a reflection that is smaller and right side up.

Back   **Front**

Images in a convex mirror

An image reflected by a convex mirror is always right side up and small no matter how far away the object is. Because convex mirrors generate a wider field of view *(right)* than do flat mirrors, they are useful as rearview mirrors in cars.

How Does a Magnifying Glass Work?

A magnifying glass consists of a double convex lens, which curves outward on both sides. Rays of light passing through the lens bend inward, converging at a focal point on either side of the lens. The distance from the center of the lens to the focal point, about 5 inches for a typical magnifying glass, is called the focal length. When a magnifying glass is held over an object at a shorter distance than the focal length, the object will appear right side up and magnified. This kind of image is called a virtual image. At a distance equal to or longer than the focal length, the lens produces an inverted image, called a real image.

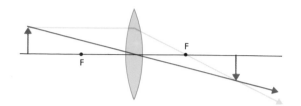

At a distance of twice the focal length from the lens, the object *(purple arrow pointing upward)* appears as a real image that is life-size but inverted.

When an object *(solid arrow)* is closer to the lens than the focal point (F) is, the lens creates a virtual image *(purple dashes)* that is right side up and magnified.

Convex lenses

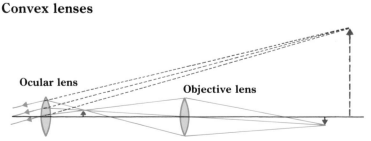

Ocular lens

Objective lens

Many telescopes use two double convex lenses, called the objective and the ocular lens. The objective lens creates a virtual image that is magnified for viewing by the ocular lens.

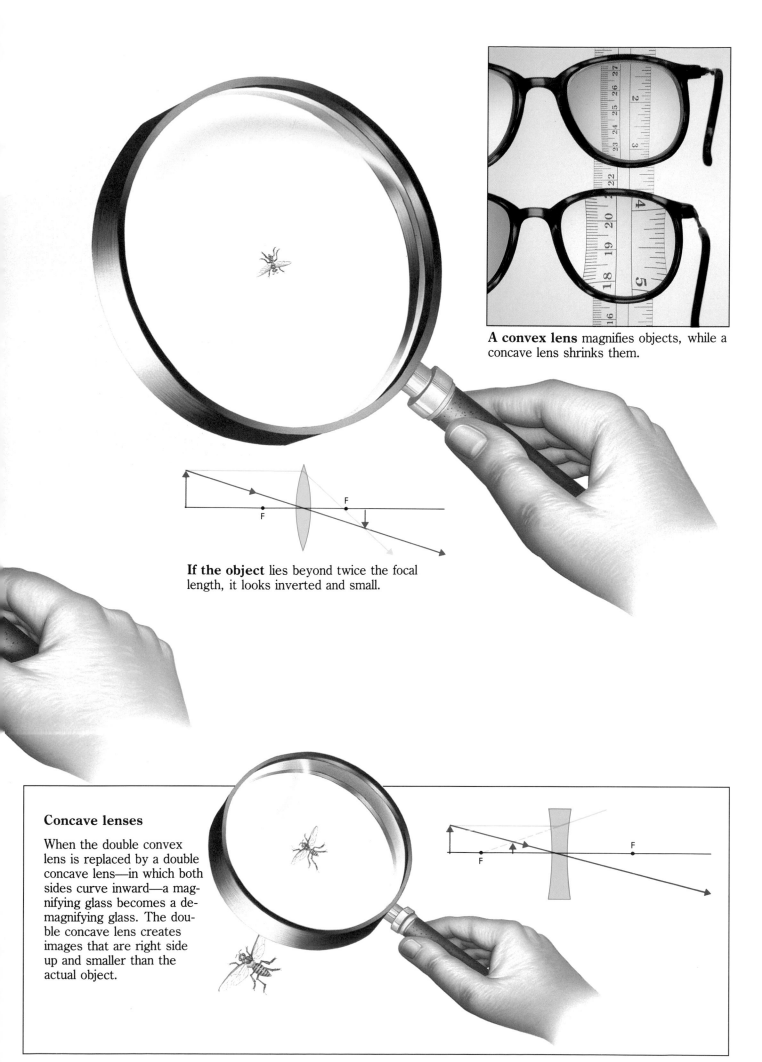

A convex lens magnifies objects, while a concave lens shrinks them.

If the object lies beyond twice the focal length, it looks inverted and small.

Concave lenses

When the double convex lens is replaced by a double concave lens—in which both sides curve inward—a magnifying glass becomes a demagnifying glass. The double concave lens creates images that are right side up and smaller than the actual object.

How Is the Speed of Light Measured?

In 1676, Danish astronomer Ole Rømer made the first rough estimate of the speed of light. Rømer noticed a slight discrepancy in the length of eclipses of the moons of Jupiter and concluded that the motion of the Earth, either approaching or receding from Jupiter, changed the distance that the light from the moons had to travel. From the discrepancy, he concluded that the speed of light was 136,646 miles per second. In a later experiment in 1849, French physicist Armand Fizeau measured the speed of light as 194,410 miles per second.

As illustrated below, Fizeau's experiment consisted of a light source, a semitransparent mirror—which reflects only half the light that strikes it, allowing the rest to pass through—and a rotating cogwheel and stationary mirror. As light struck the semitransparent mirror, it reflected toward the cogwheel, which sliced it into beams. Kept in tight focus by lenses placed along its path, each beam reflected off the stationary mirror and back toward the cogwheel. By measuring the precise speed at which the cogwheel blocked the beams, Fizeau could calculate the speed of light. His colleague Jean Foucault refined this method a year later, arriving at a speed of light of 185,093 miles per second. This figure was close to the modern value of 186,282 miles per second, which is calculated by multiplying the wavelength and frequency of a laser beam.

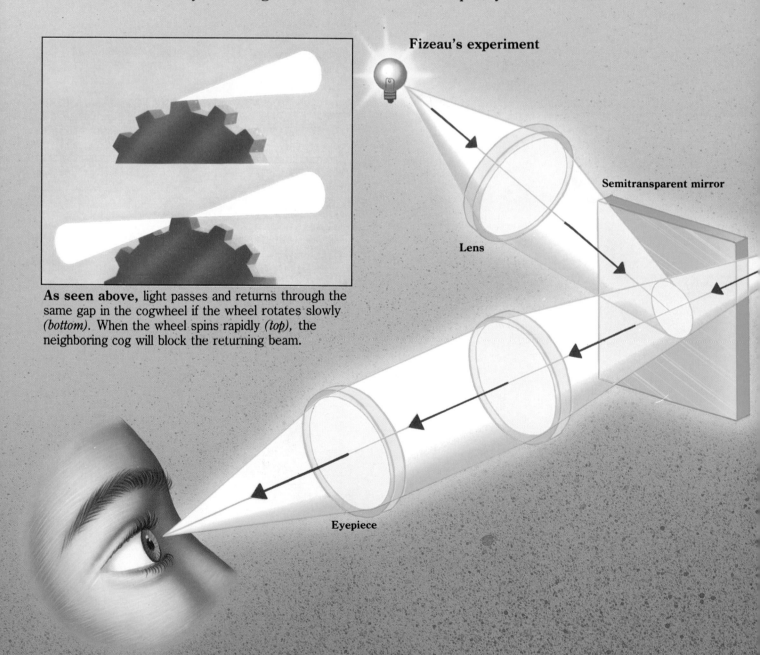

Fizeau's experiment

Semitransparent mirror

Lens

Eyepiece

As seen above, light passes and returns through the same gap in the cogwheel if the wheel rotates slowly *(bottom)*. When the wheel spins rapidly *(top)*, the neighboring cog will block the returning beam.

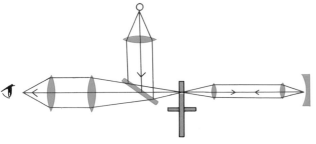
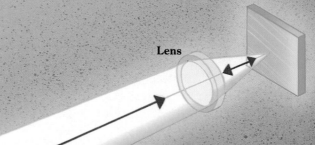

Lens

Lens

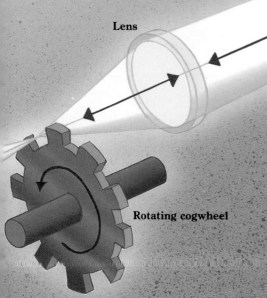

Rotating cogwheel

Closing the book on the speed of light. The invention of lasers *(pages 122-123)* enabled physicists to measure the speed of light with greater accuracy than ever before. In 1972, scientists of the National Institute of Standards and Technology carefully determined the wavelength and frequency of a laser beam and fixed the speed of light, the product of these two variables, at 299,792,458 meters per second, or 186,282 miles per second. One consequence of this new measure was a decision by the General Conference of Weights and Measures to fix the meter, or 3.3 feet, as the distance light travels in $\frac{1}{299,792,458}$ of a second. As a result, the speed of light, the most important fundamental constant in physics, now is calculated with certainty, and the meter can be defined far more accurately than was once possible.

Foucault's experiment

In 1850, French physicist Jean Foucault modified Fizeau's technique by substituting a rotating mirror for the cogwheel. Only when the mirror makes a complete 360° revolution between the time of the light beam's departure and return does an observer detect any light from the source. This method let Foucault calculate a value of 185,093 miles per second for the speed of light.

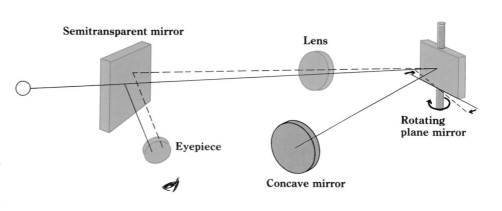

Semitransparent mirror

Lens

Eyepiece

Concave mirror

Rotating plane mirror

Why Are Soap Bubbles So Colorful?

The kaleidoscope of colors swirling across a soap bubble is caused by the complex nature of light and the way it reflects off the bubble's surface. White light consists of an array of colors, each characterized by a different wavelength, shown at right as waves with crests and troughs. When light strikes the surface of a soap bubble, some light waves immediately reflect off the bubble. Other waves penetrate the film of the bubble itself, where they bend and reflect off the inner surface. When these waves meet up with waves bouncing off the outer surface, their crests and troughs are not always aligned. When crests and troughs match up, the waves strengthen each other. But when they do not match, they weaken each other in so-called wave interference. In such a case, a rainbow appears on the soap film because varying thicknesses in the film cause interference patterns and reflect light in the different wavelengths of each color.

The spectrum of white light

When white light passes through a prism *(below),* the light breaks into its component colors, the familiar red, orange, yellow, green, blue, indigo, and violet of the rainbow. Shorter wavelengths refract at greater angles than longer wavelengths. Violet, with the shortest wavelength, bends the most, while red, with the longest wavelength, bends least.

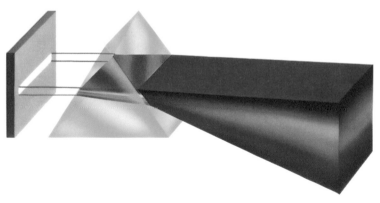

Interference in a film of oil

On a thin oil film, colors result from interference, depending on the film's thickness and the angle at which the light strikes *(below).* Black appears where all light waves cancel each other out.

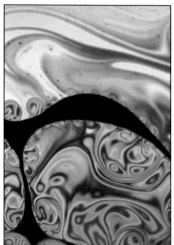

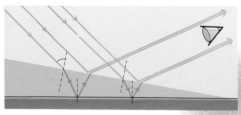

Swirls of color appear on an oil film.

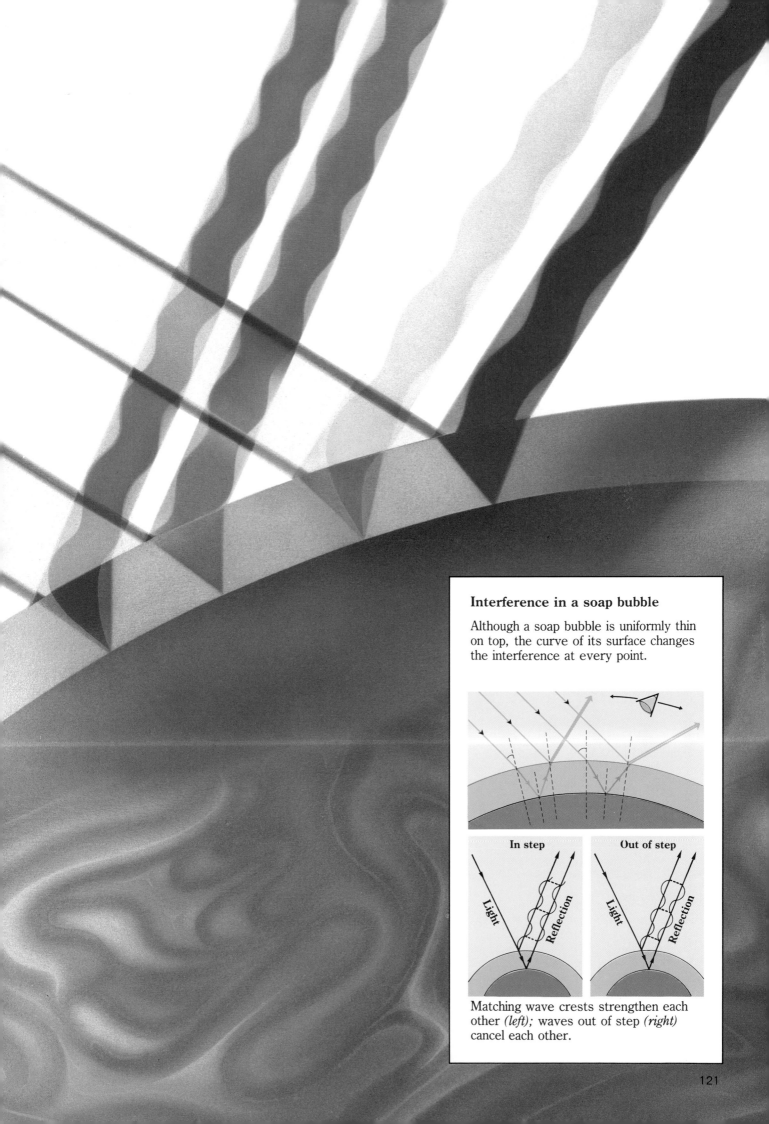

Interference in a soap bubble

Although a soap bubble is uniformly thin on top, the curve of its surface changes the interference at every point.

In step

Light

Reflection

Out of step

Light

Reflection

Matching wave crests strengthen each other *(left);* waves out of step *(right)* cancel each other.

What Is a Laser?

The laser is a device that produces a narrow beam of intense light. Lasers exploit the fact that the electrons in an atom can only occupy specific orbits around their nucleus. When an atom receives a jolt of energy, it can become excited, pushing its electrons from the lowest energy orbit, called the ground state, to one of higher energy. But the electrons cannot stay long in a high-energy orbit and begin to drop back down to the ground state, each emitting a photon, or wave of light, in the process. Once one atom starts, it triggers a chain reaction of other electrons dropping down, resulting in an avalanche of identical light waves perfectly aligned with one another. These waves form a powerful beam that in some lasers grows strong enough to cut through stone and metal. Invented in 1960, lasers are used in fields as varied as medicine, to vaporize tumors, and music, to etch and read the signals on compact disks.

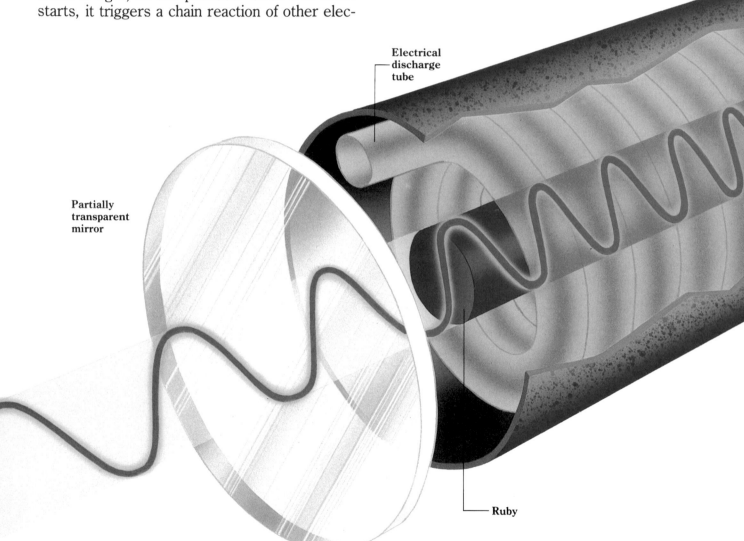

Electrical discharge tube

Partially transparent mirror

Ruby

A sharper focus

A laser beam contains just one wavelength of light and can be tightly focused at a single point by a lens *(right)*. Natural light with several wavelengths does not focus as sharply *(far right)*. What makes the laser an important tool is its ability to focus a lot of energy on a tiny spot and to travel long distances at low power without spreading and weakening as multicolored light does.

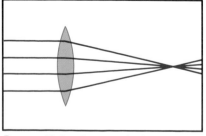

Laser light (one color)

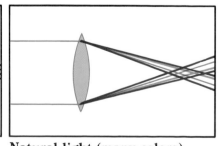

Natural light (many colors)

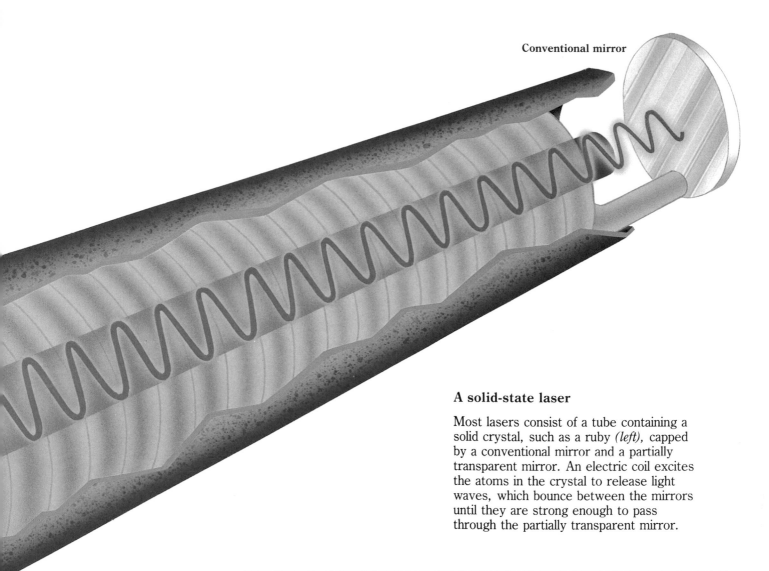

Conventional mirror

A solid-state laser

Most lasers consist of a tube containing a solid crystal, such as a ruby *(left),* capped by a conventional mirror and a partially transparent mirror. An electric coil excites the atoms in the crystal to release light waves, which bounce between the mirrors until they are strong enough to pass through the partially transparent mirror.

Building a laser beam

1. The electrons of each atom *(black dots on inner circles, right)* reside in the ground state before the laser is turned on.

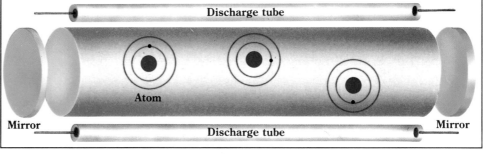

2. Once the laser is switched on, energy from the discharge tube pushes the electrons into more energetic orbits *(outer circles).*

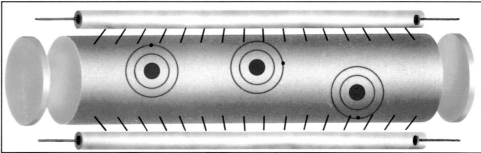

3. As electrons start falling back to the ground state, they emit light, prompting other electrons to do the same. The resulting beam has one wavelength and grows stronger as more electrons drop down.

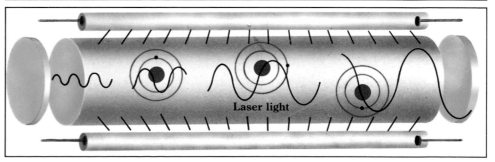

123

What Is a Hologram?

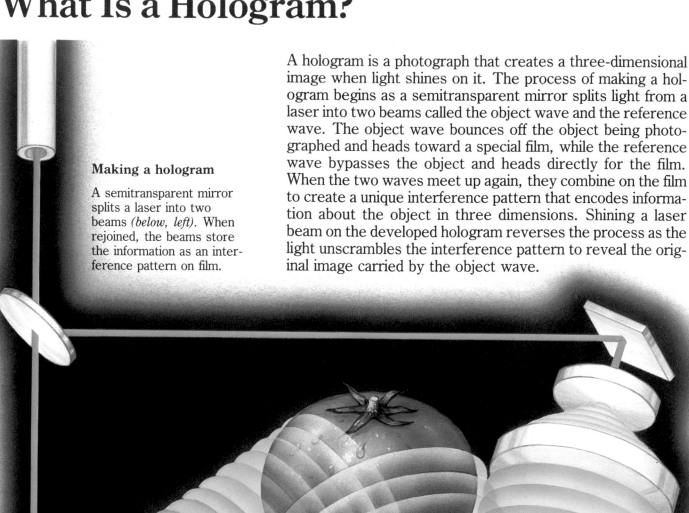

Making a hologram

A semitransparent mirror splits a laser into two beams *(below, left)*. When rejoined, the beams store the information as an interference pattern on film.

A hologram is a photograph that creates a three-dimensional image when light shines on it. The process of making a hologram begins as a semitransparent mirror splits light from a laser into two beams called the object wave and the reference wave. The object wave bounces off the object being photographed and heads toward a special film, while the reference wave bypasses the object and heads directly for the film. When the two waves meet up again, they combine on the film to create a unique interference pattern that encodes information about the object in three dimensions. Shining a laser beam on the developed hologram reverses the process as the light unscrambles the interference pattern to reveal the original image carried by the object wave.

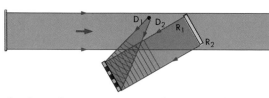

An interference pattern forms as object waves, D_1 and D_2, and reference waves, R_1 and R_2, meet at different angles. Areas of constructive, or mutually strengthening, interference appear in black on the diagram.

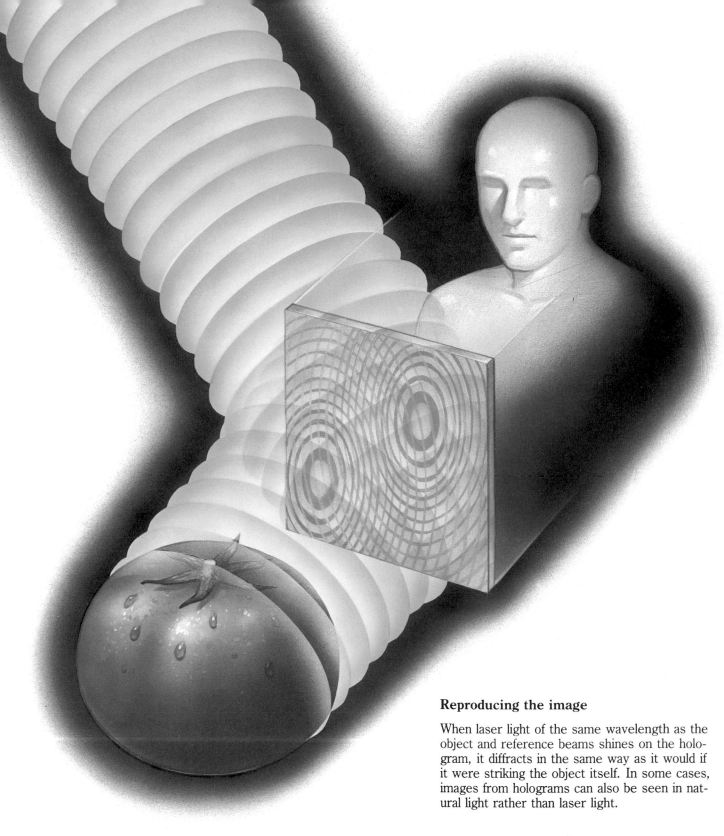

Reproducing the image

When laser light of the same wavelength as the object and reference beams shines on the hologram, it diffracts in the same way as it would if it were striking the object itself. In some cases, images from holograms can also be seen in natural light rather than laser light.

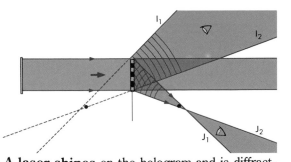

A laser shines on the hologram and is diffracted as I_1, I_2 or J_1, J_2 by the interference on the film, re-creating a three-dimensional image.

Image in the round

A natural-light image

What Happens near the Speed of Light?

In 1887, American scientists Albert Michelson and Edward Morley performed an experiment that proved the speed of light is constant for every observer. Building on that experiment, Albert Einstein stated in his special theory of relativity two decades later that nothing except light itself can travel at the speed of light, 186,282 miles per second. But for objects traveling very close to the speed of light, very strange things would happen. Time would slow down for an object approaching the speed of light relative to time experienced by an observer on Earth. The object's length would shrink, and its mass would increase. If not for the speed limit imposed by relativity, a rocket traveling at the speed of light would have zero length and infinite mass—both impossible results.

Einstein's theory does have some interesting consequences for future space travelers. Inside a spaceship traveling close to the speed of light everything would seem normal. But to an observer on Earth the ship would look shorter and its clocks would be slow. Astronauts spending, by their reckoning, a decade hurtling through space might return to find that a century had passed on Earth.

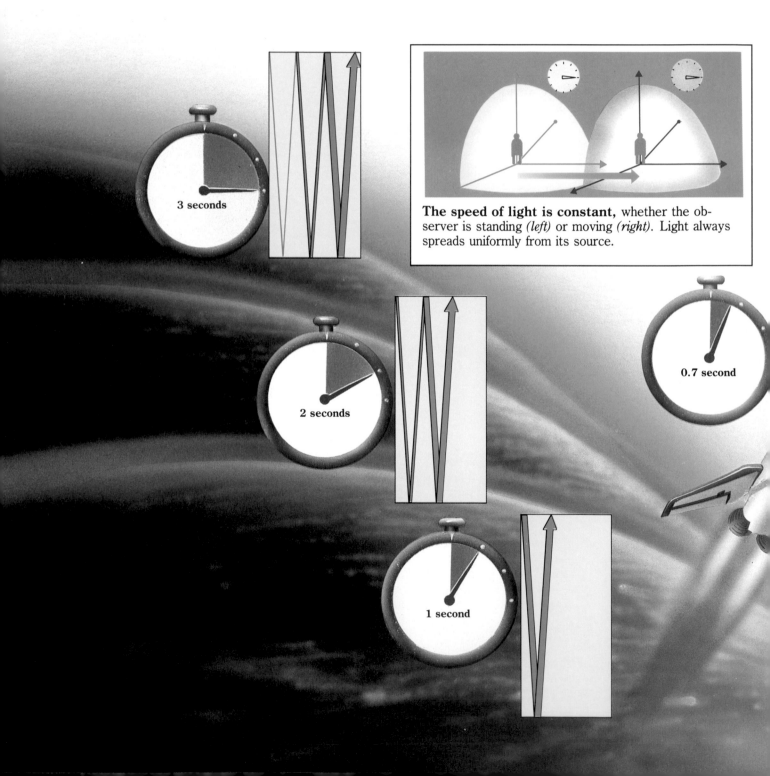

The speed of light is constant, whether the observer is standing *(left)* or moving *(right)*. Light always spreads uniformly from its source.

3 seconds

2 seconds

1 second

0.7 second

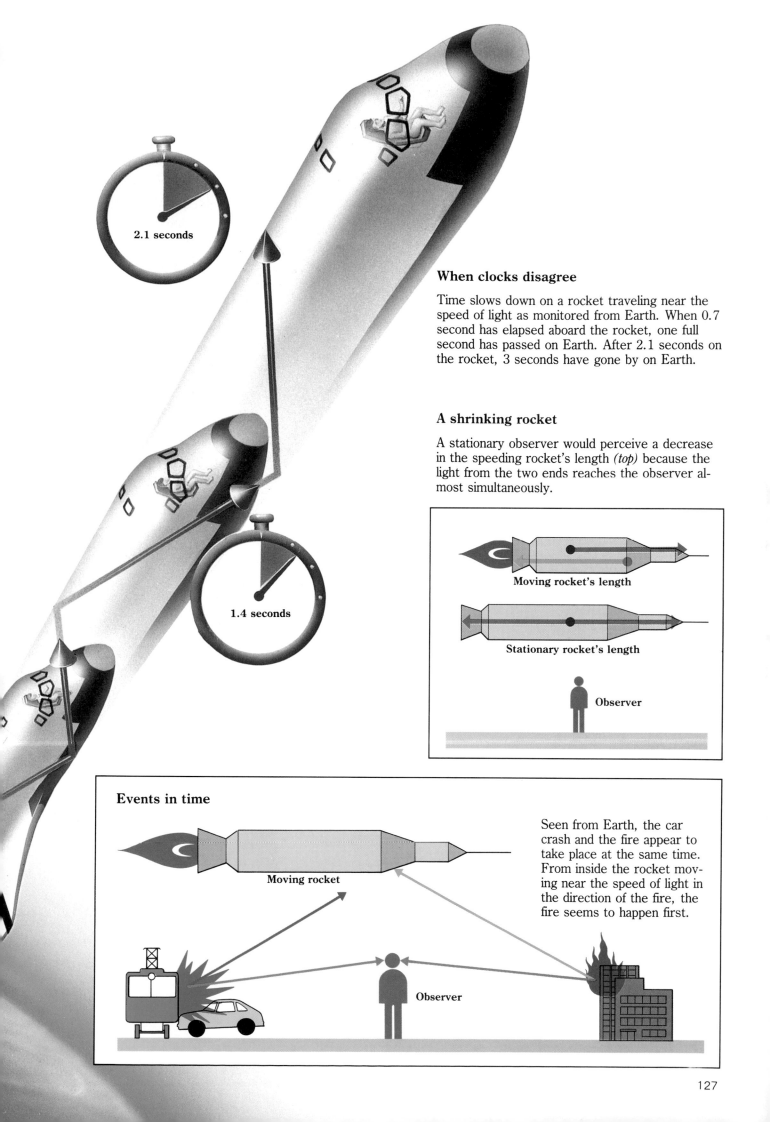

2.1 seconds

1.4 seconds

When clocks disagree

Time slows down on a rocket traveling near the speed of light as monitored from Earth. When 0.7 second has elapsed aboard the rocket, one full second has passed on Earth. After 2.1 seconds on the rocket, 3 seconds have gone by on Earth.

A shrinking rocket

A stationary observer would perceive a decrease in the speeding rocket's length *(top)* because the light from the two ends reaches the observer almost simultaneously.

Moving rocket's length

Stationary rocket's length

Observer

Events in time

Moving rocket

Seen from Earth, the car crash and the fire appear to take place at the same time. From inside the rocket moving near the speed of light in the direction of the fire, the fire seems to happen first.

Observer

8

The Physics of Sound

The world is teeming with sounds, ranging from barely audible rumblings to piercing shrieks. Soft or loud, soothing or shattering, the phenomenon of sound gives people invaluable clues about their environment. Sound owes its existence to waves produced by subtle vibrations of an object, such as a snare drum that has been struck. These waves are transmitted through air and other gases, liquids, and solids. When they reach a person's ear, the waves are perceived differently according to their characteristics.

A key factor is frequency, defined as the rate at which successive crests or troughs of a series of waves pass a fixed point in space. Frequency is expressed in terms of hertz, representing a count of one wave cycle per second. Humans can hear sounds in the 20 to 20,000 hertz range. A wave's frequency is related to a sound's pitch, with high-frequency waves yielding high pitch and low frequencies producing low pitch. Scientists measure a sound's intensity, which depends on a wave's inherent energy, with a standard unit called a decibel. Normal conversation registers about 60 decibels, a jet engine 140 to 160. Sounds above 120 decibels may result in damage to the eardrums and possibly a total loss of hearing.

Each instrument shown at right has its own distinctive timbre, or quality of sound. By striking a surface, blowing into a mouthpiece, or plucking or bowing strings, musicians make music, producing sound waves of different pitches.

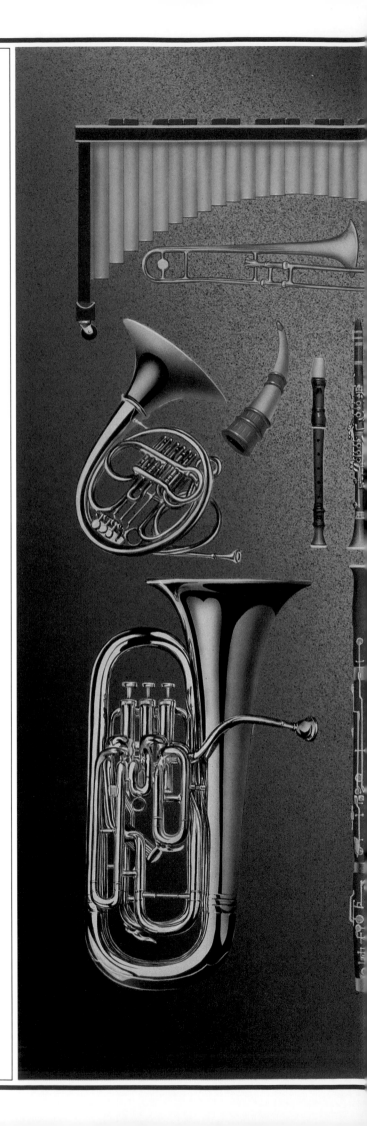

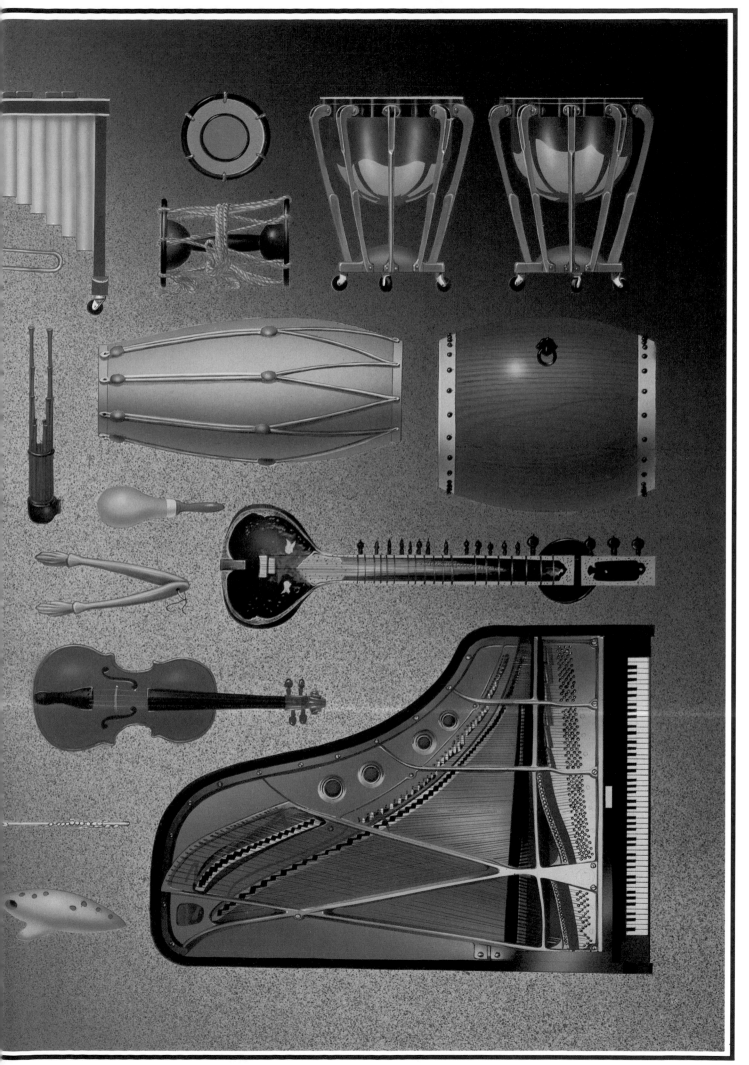

How Is Sound Transmitted?

Sound is transmitted by waves. These waves travel through gases, liquids, and solids alike. Wave action is mainly a transfer of energy. In the case of sound, this transfer takes the form of tiny motions at the molecular level. In gases and liquids, a sound wave shifts molecules slightly in a direction parallel to itself, that is, in a lengthwise direction. In solids, motion may also occur perpendicular to the wave.

Sound waves spread from their source in all directions, as depicted at right, where a metal bell has been struck by its clapper. This mechanical jarring has made the bell vibrate. The energy of the vibrations stirs surrounding molecules of air, pushing them away from the bell. This slight expansion of the air surrounding the bell results in an increase in pressure, which propagates outward from the source.

The speed of sound is independent of loudness of tone. The sounds from a radio in a room, whether they are loud or soft, of high pitch or low, all reach a listener simultaneously.

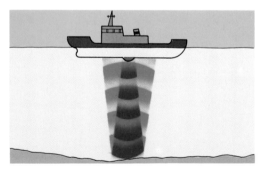

Sounding the depths

Sonar beams, made up of sound waves, pass easily through ocean water. Sonar relies on the fact that sound waves reflect off the ocean floor; it is used to "sense" the presence of underwater features.

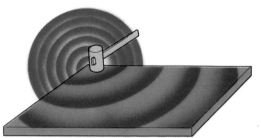

Elastic solids

Sound travels through a sheet of wood. The molecules of most solids are linked in a tight framework that is not easily compressed but hastens the passage of sound waves.

The speed of sound varies depending on the medium it passes through and the medium's temperature. Sound waves travel slowly through a gas because its loose molecular structure is easily compressed. The speed increases in liquids and becomes even faster in solids, as shown below in meters per second (m/s).

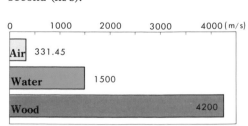

	0	1000	2000	3000	4000 (m/s)
Air	331.45				
Water		1500			
Wood					4200

Ringing the bell

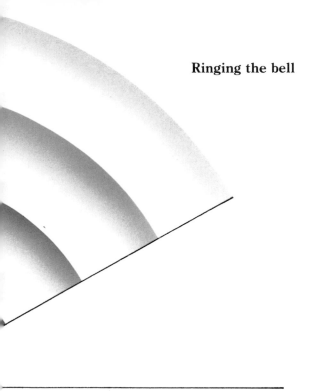

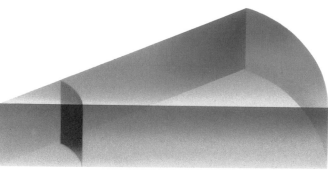

A sonic wave front moves outward from a vibrating bell.

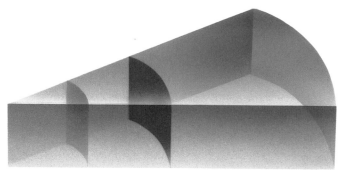

It proceeds at a constant rate through evenly heated air.

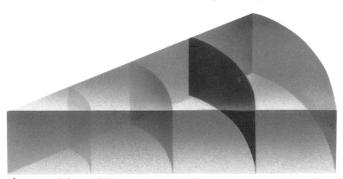

A second front follows at a set distance, or wavelength.

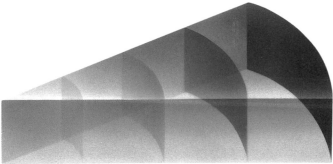

Waves are strongest near the source.

The way of the wave

Sound waves spread through the air as in the diagrams at right. Wave fronts move outward at given distances keyed to the bell's frequency. A sound wave's frequency is determined by counting the number of wave fronts passing a given point in a given time.

Portraying an invisible wave

A simple sound wave passing through air is represented graphically as a wavy line *(right)*. The crests of the wave represent molecular compression; the troughs, the elastic expansion that takes place after the wave front has passed. The more complex a sound, the more intermediate crests and troughs the wave-form portraying it has. Loud sounds bearing great energies show high wave heights, or amplitudes.

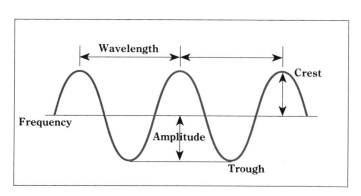

What Causes Echoes?

Echoes result when sound waves moving outward from a source—so-called incident waves—run into a solid barrier such as the face of a mountain. Sound waves reflect from, or bounce off, such obstacles at an angle equal to that at which they have struck.

The distance of the barrier from the origin of the sound is a key factor. When the barrier is nearby, the reflected waves make the return trip rapidly enough to mingle with the original waves, and no echo is formed. If the barrier stands at least 50 feet away, the reflected waves will not return until after the incident waves have stopped. Then listeners will hear the sound repeated as if it is coming from the direction of the barrier. Acoustical engineers must plan auditoriums and concert halls with echoes in mind, adding soundproofing and eliminating structural features that might prove overly reflective.

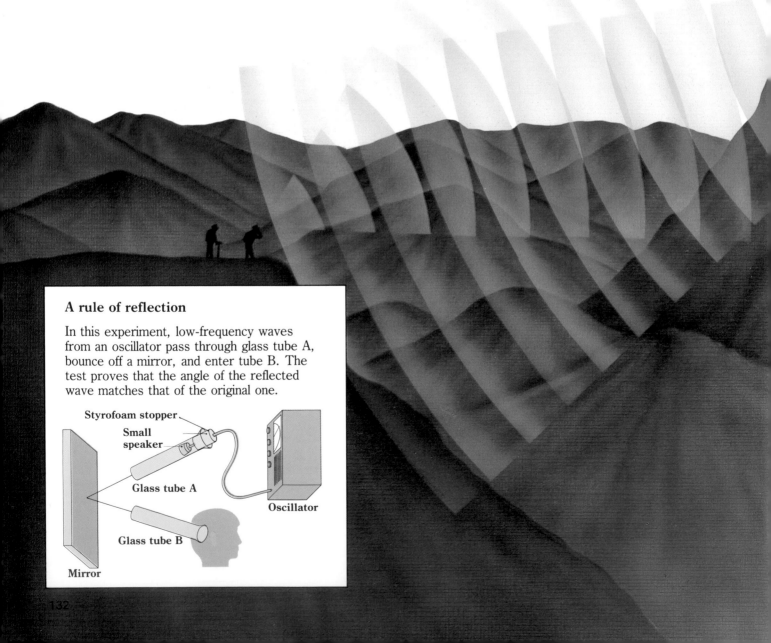

A rule of reflection

In this experiment, low-frequency waves from an oscillator pass through glass tube A, bounce off a mirror, and enter tube B. The test proves that the angle of the reflected wave matches that of the original one.

Styrofoam stopper

Small speaker

Glass tube A

Oscillator

Glass tube B

Mirror

Speedy by day

Sound speeds through warm air near the ground (*below*) but slows when reaching cooler upper layers. The change results in upward refraction, or bending, of the wave.

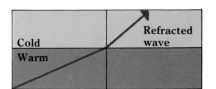

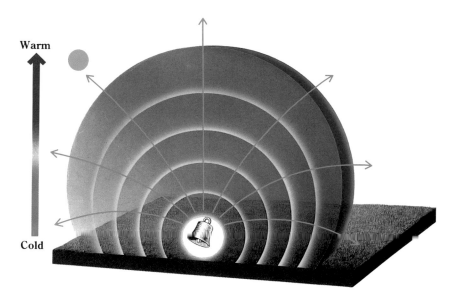

Slow by night

Cool nighttime ground temperatures slow the passage of sound (*below*). Warmer overlying layers increase the speed of sound.

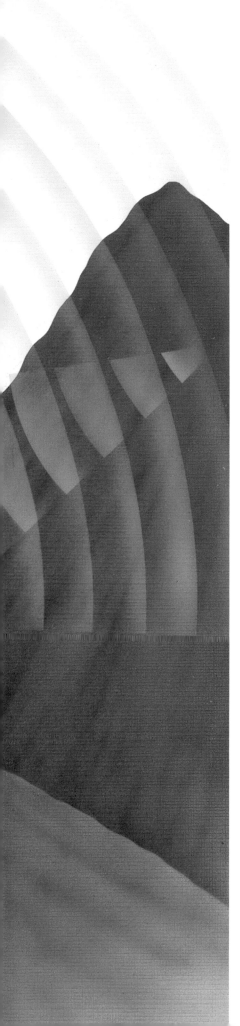

Sound travels with the wind

Wind moves more rapidly far above the ground than near the ground. When sound waves spread out from the ground, they travel with the wind. An upwind listener would hear only a faint sound; a downwind listener would hear the bell from far away.

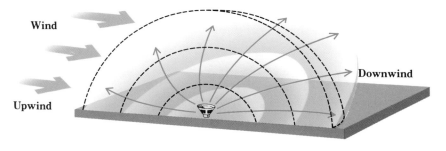

How Are Tones Produced?

Musicians coax tones, or notes of various pitches, from instruments by controlling their sound-producing vibrations. When a violinist pulls the bow across a string, the string begins to vibrate, or oscillate. Waves travel up and down the string's length, forming patterns called standing waves. Similarly, when the player of a recorder blows into the mouthpiece, standing waves form in the column of air inside the recorder. Each wave produces a different tone. The lowest note a string or an air column can produce is called the fundamental tone. Any time that note is sounded, higher pitches, called overtones, are also produced; this occurs when a fundamental wave breaks up into sections. The distinctive sound, or timbre, of an instrument is caused by the relative strength or weakness of overtones.

A singing string

A violin string oscillates at a fundamental frequency as shown below. An image of the sound can be viewed on an oscilloscope as a complex wave pattern *(bottom)* typical for stringed instruments.

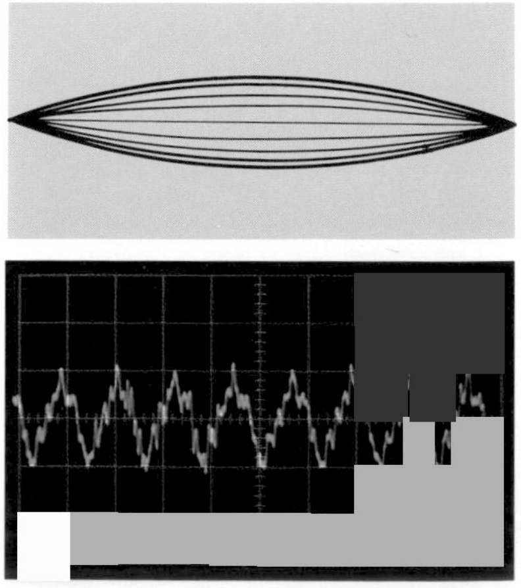

The king of strings

The violin's wooden body is the key to its elegant timbre. When bowed or plucked, the strings vibrate, causing the carved and varnished panels of the instrument to resonate, or vibrate, at the same frequency. This amplifies the sound, so it is loud enough to be heard.

Violin meets recorder

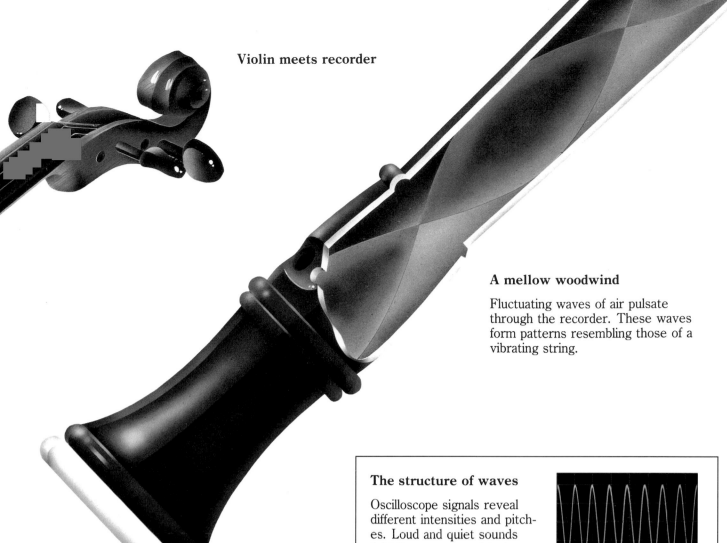

A mellow woodwind

Fluctuating waves of air pulsate through the recorder. These waves form patterns resembling those of a vibrating string.

The structure of waves

Oscilloscope signals reveal different intensities and pitches. Loud and quiet sounds (*right*) are measured in terms of decibels. People most readily detect waves between 1 and 120 decibels. High and low pitches (*below, right*) are related to frequency, the rate at which crests or troughs of a wave pass a given point.

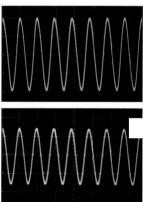

Loud and soft sounds

A wave machine

An oscilloscope graphs the wave-forms of sounds. High-pitch/high-frequency sounds have short wavelengths; low-pitch/low-frequency sounds have long wavelengths.

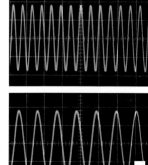

High and low pitches

Sound waves can be viewed on an oscilloscope screen.

The sound of breath

Overtones appear as divisions in a standing wave in the air column below. At bottom is the relatively simple signature of this sound wave. Woodwinds have a smooth, direct sound.

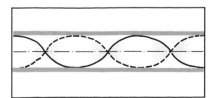

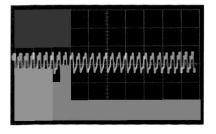

What Is the Doppler Effect?

The Doppler effect is the well-known change in sound that occurs when the source of a sound is moving in relation to a listener. To the stationary listener, the sound appears to rise gradually in pitch as the source of the sound approaches and then to fall as it continues past the listener. This so-called Doppler shift is caused by sound wave fronts that arrive in ever-greater frequency as the moving object nears the listener. The increase in frequency is accompanied by a shrinking of wavelength. As scientists are aware, the higher the frequency of a sound, the higher its pitch. When the object moves away from the listener, the reverse takes place. Frequency drops, wavelength increases, and the apparent tone of the sound that the listener hears becomes lower and lower.

The Doppler effect can be commonly heard in passing train whistles, ambulance or police sirens, and jet plane engines.

An arriving train whistles shrilly.

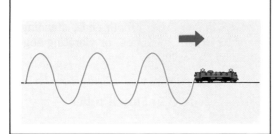

A receding train

As the train moves away, wave fronts of its whistle take longer to reach a listener, who hears a drop in pitch.

An illusion bred by motion

To a listener on a train, the pitch of its whistle is constant. But to listeners behind or in front of the train *(above, right)*, the pitch shifts because of the uneven spacing of wave fronts.

An alternate view

Another way of considering the Doppler effect is to imagine a listener approaching the sound. The closer the walker comes to the bell, the faster the wave fronts reach him, and the higher pitched the tolling of the bell sounds.

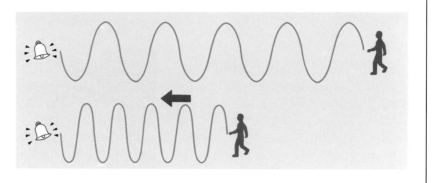

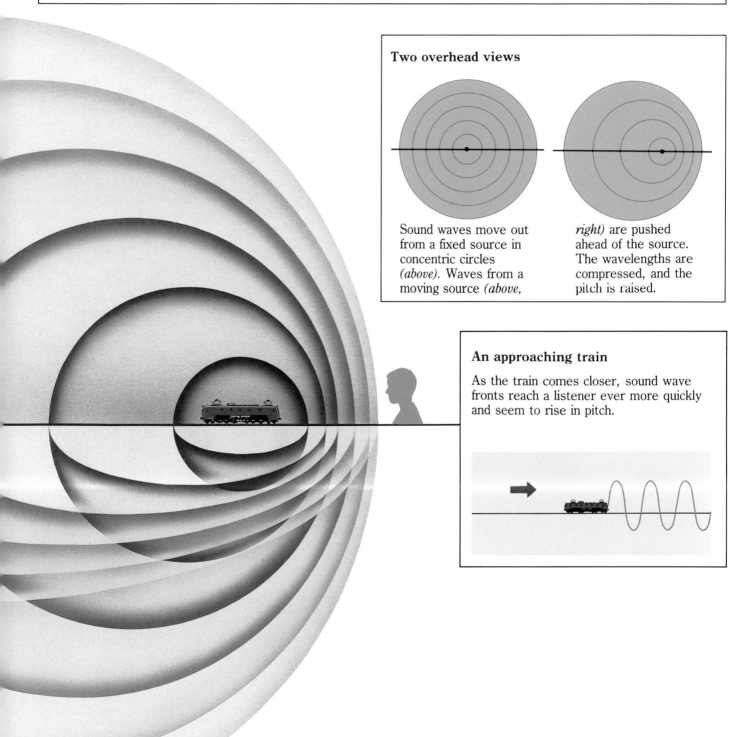

Two overhead views

Sound waves move out from a fixed source in concentric circles *(above)*. Waves from a moving source *(above,* *right)* are pushed ahead of the source. The wavelengths are compressed, and the pitch is raised.

An approaching train

As the train comes closer, sound wave fronts reach a listener ever more quickly and seem to rise in pitch.

What Is a Sonic Boom?

A sonic boom is the thunderous noise that fills the sky when an airplane flies faster than the speed of sound, breaking through the sound barrier. As the aircraft accelerates to this speed, called mach 1, it compresses the atmosphere in front of and beside it. (Mach 1 occurs at different speeds because the speed of sound varies; at sea level and a temperature of 32° F., sound travels 343 meters, or 1,100 feet, per second.)

After the jet passes, the air expands again. The higher the speed of the passing plane, the more pent-up energy will be released in this expansion. When the plane flies at supersonic speeds, that is, faster than mach 1, the expansion takes place so rapidly that the molecules collide with relatively still surrounding air, thereby creating a sonic boom and powerful shock waves. These shock waves ripple outward in a widening cone. If the plane is close to the ground when the boom comes, as shown at right, the shock waves intersect with the ground. They are strong enough to damage structures, sometimes shattering glass and cracking walls.

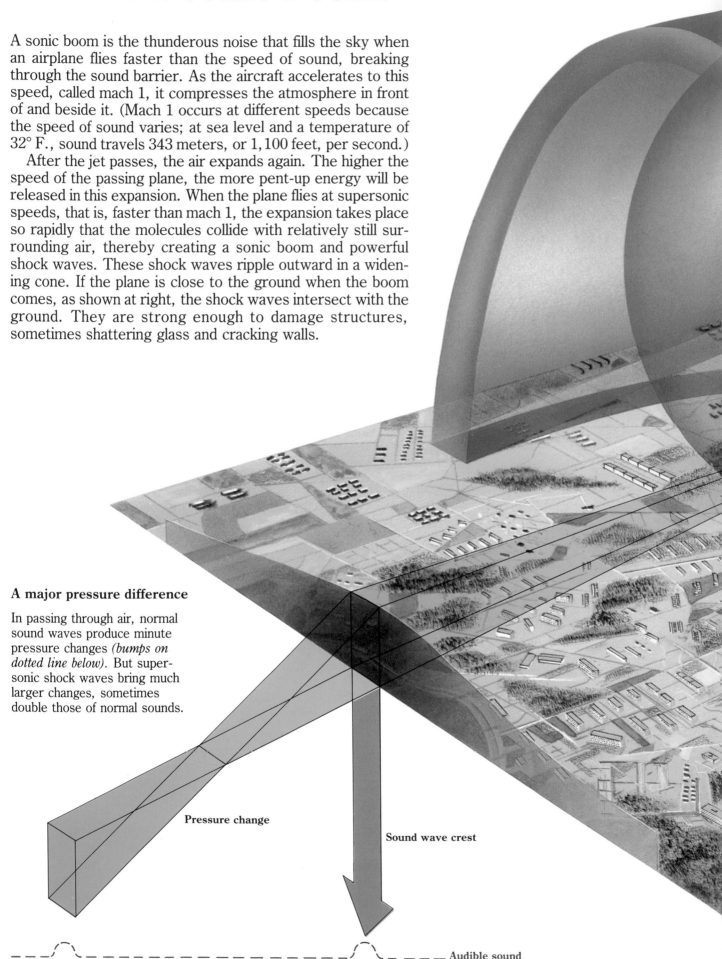

A major pressure difference

In passing through air, normal sound waves produce minute pressure changes *(bumps on dotted line below)*. But supersonic shock waves bring much larger changes, sometimes double those of normal sounds.

Pressure change

Sound wave crest

Audible sound

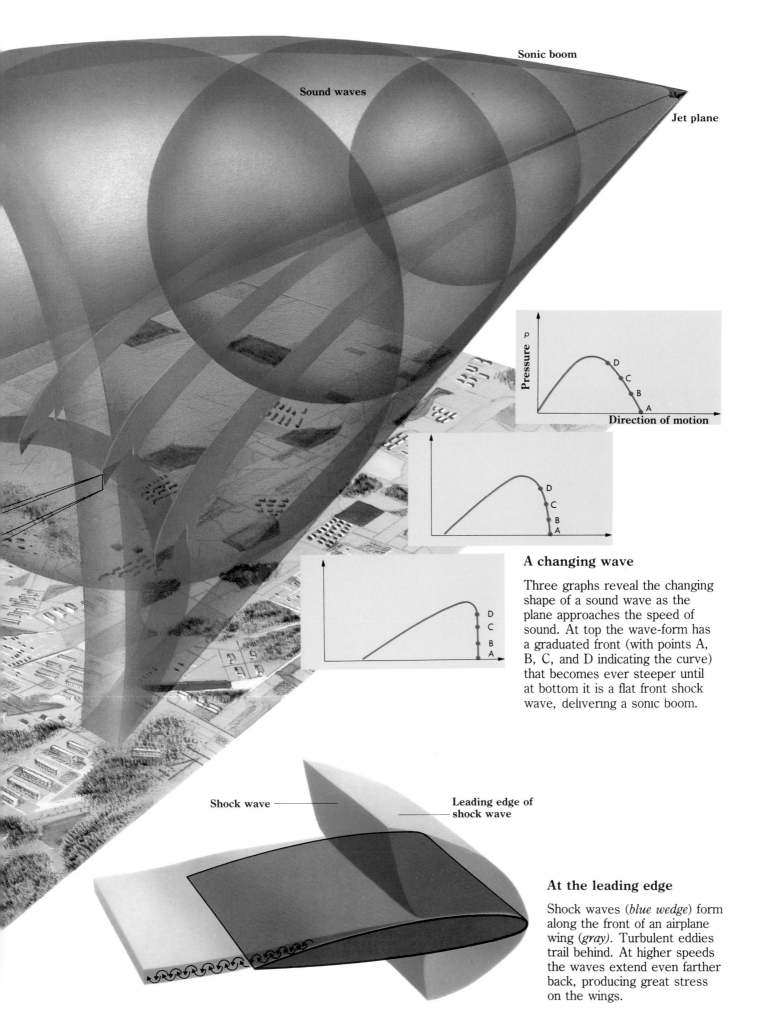

Sonic boom

Sound waves

Jet plane

A changing wave

Three graphs reveal the changing shape of a sound wave as the plane approaches the speed of sound. At top the wave-form has a graduated front (with points A, B, C, and D indicating the curve) that becomes ever steeper until at bottom it is a flat front shock wave, delivering a sonic boom.

Shock wave

Leading edge of shock wave

At the leading edge

Shock waves (*blue wedge*) form along the front of an airplane wing (*gray*). Turbulent eddies trail behind. At higher speeds the waves extend even farther back, producing great stress on the wings.

How Are Musical Instruments Tuned?

At the beginning of a concert, musicians in a symphony orchestra tune their instruments to a single note played by the oboist. With all the instruments in tune, they can be assured of harmony. But when an instrument such as a piano gets out of tune, a more elaborate procedure is required. Then, trained technicians must tighten or loosen the wires for each key so that its pitch exactly matches that of the appropriate tuning fork. Tuning forks are highly precise tools that yield specific pitches when they are set to vibrating. For example, forks designed to vibrate at 262 hertz, or units of frequency, produce the note middle C on the eight-note musical scale, while those at 440 hertz produce the note A in the same octave, called middle A, and those at 524, the note C one octave above middle C. The frequencies of notes an octave apart are related. The higher note vibrates at exactly twice the rate of the lower one. An expert tuner can tell when the piano note precisely matches that of the tuning fork. When the two differ, their sound waves interact in such a way that a pulsing hum, called a beat, is heard. When this humming vanishes, the key is in tune.

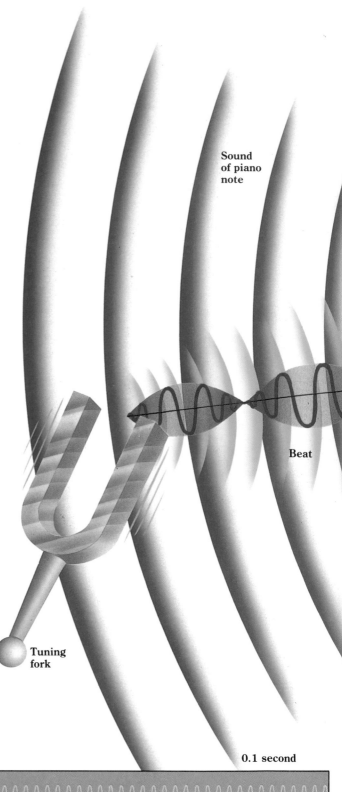

Sound of piano note

Beat

Tuning fork

0.1 second

Bringing notes into line

The tuning fork vibrates at 440 hertz, the piano's out-of-tune A key at 520 hertz. When the two interact *(third and fourth band)*, a fluctuating wave results. Once the pitches are the same *(bottom band)*, the sound becomes steady.

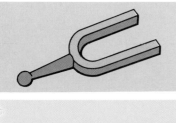

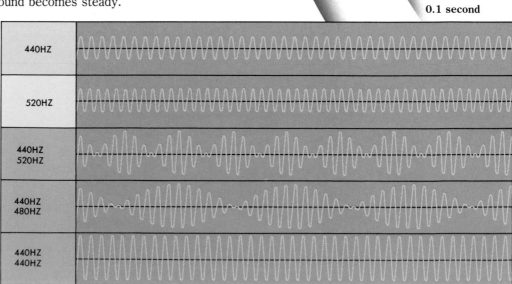

440HZ	
520HZ	
440HZ 520HZ	
440HZ 480HZ	
440HZ 440HZ	

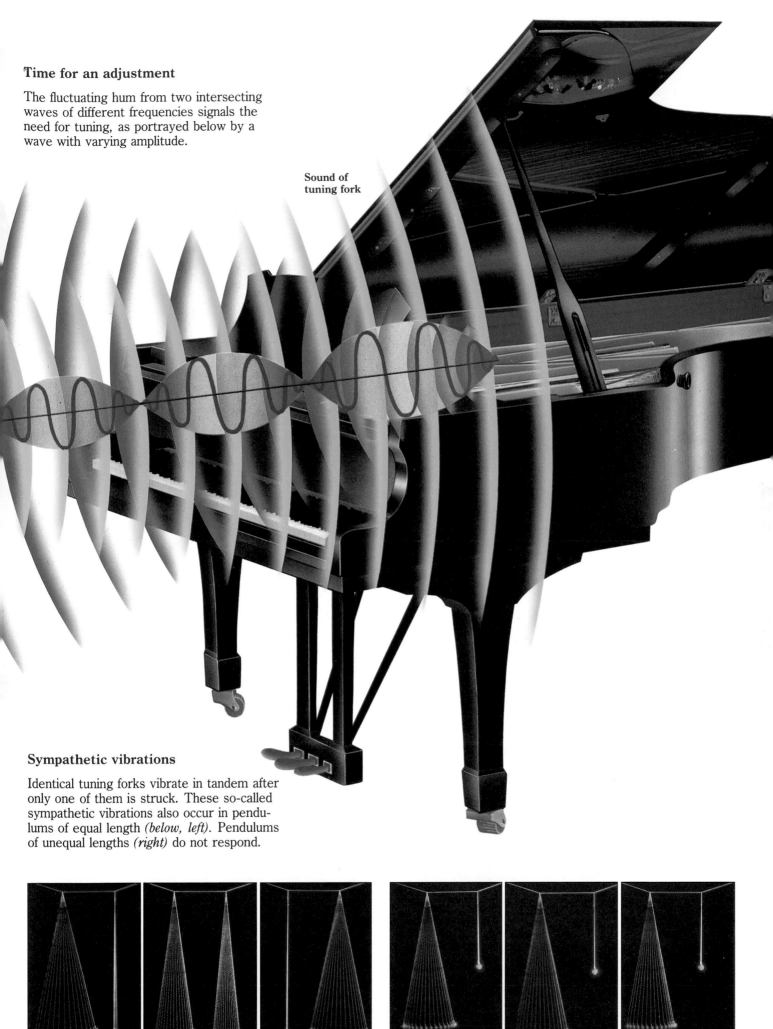

Time for an adjustment

The fluctuating hum from two intersecting waves of different frequencies signals the need for tuning, as portrayed below by a wave with varying amplitude.

Sound of
tuning fork

Sympathetic vibrations

Identical tuning forks vibrate in tandem after only one of them is struck. These so-called sympathetic vibrations also occur in pendulums of equal length *(below, left)*. Pendulums of unequal lengths *(right)* do not respond.

What Is a Surround-Sound System?

A surround-sound system simulates the acoustical experience of being in a concert hall for listeners in a small room. This impression relies on special recordings, which are computer-adjusted to carry separate sound tracks for four channels feeding into left front, left rear, right front, and right rear speakers. Digital processors allow recording engineers to eliminate some sounds and enhance others. This lets engineers take pure sound waves from instruments and combine them with the effects of waves being reflected off and absorbed by the walls of a concert hall. The resulting recording carries enough information to surround a listener with sound.

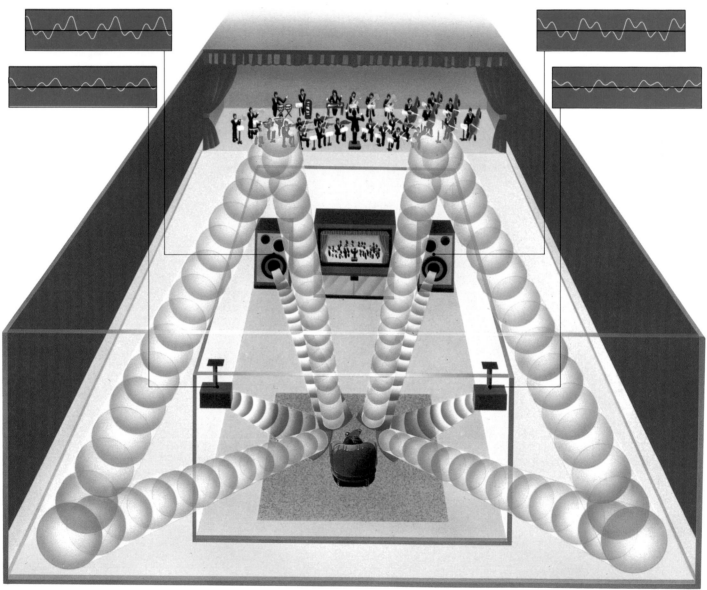

The surround-sound signal

A surround-sound track consists of two signals: the sum of the output from a pair of microphones, and their difference—sound from one but not the other.

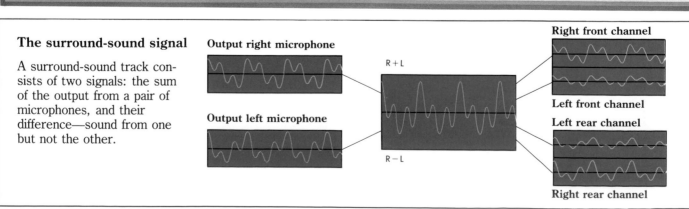

Output right microphone

Output left microphone

R + L

R − L

Right front channel

Left front channel

Left rear channel

Right rear channel

Glossary

Aerodynamics: The study of the forces that act on objects moving through air.

Airfoil: Any object, such as an airplane wing, designed to generate lift when moving through air.

Alpha particle: A particle consisting of two protons and two neutrons, released by atomic nuclei during radioactive decay.

Alternating current: Electric current that changes direction.

Amplitude: The height of a wave's crests.

Angular momentum: A measure of an object's rotational energy; its value depends on the object's spin rate and mass.

Antinode: A point along a standing wave that has a maximum amplitude.

Atmospheric pressure: The pressure exerted by the atmosphere; at sea level the normal atmospheric pressure is equal to 14.7 pounds per square inch.

Battery: A cell consisting of a mixture of chemicals that provides an electromotive force when connected to a circuit.

Beta particle: A particle consisting of either an electron or a positron, sometimes released by atomic nuclei undergoing radioactive decay.

Boiling point: The temperature at which a substance changes from liquid to vapor.

Buoyant force: An upward force equal to the weight of a substance, such as air or water, displaced by an object.

Circuit: A closed pathway through which electric current flows. Circuits with resistors can be arranged in **parallel,** in which each resistor is attached in a separate loop in the circuit; and in a **series,** in which resistors are placed one after another.

Concave: Any object that bends inward such as the inner surface of a hollow sphere.

Condensation: The process in which vapor changes into a solid or liquid.

Conductor: Material that allows electric current to flow through.

Convection: A process in which heat circulates throughout a volume of liquid or gas.

Convex: Any object, such as a mirror or lens, that bends outward such as the outer surface of a sphere.

Density: The ratio of an object's mass to its volume.

Diffraction: The property of light by which light waves bend around the edges of any object they encounter.

Diode: A device that allows current to flow in only one direction.

Direct current: Electric current that flows in only one direction.

Doppler effect: A phenomenon in which the frequency—and thus pitch—of a sound wave increases for a listener as the source of the sound approaches and decreases as the source recedes.

Drag: The force of friction that retards the movement of an object through air.

Elastic limit: The maximum force from which a stretched or compressed spring will recover its initial shape; any applied force beyond this limit will permanently bend the spring.

Electricity: The field exerted by a charged particle; a stationary particle produces static electricity, and a moving particle produces current.

Electromagnet: A magnet made by wrapping a current-bearing wire around a ferromagnetic material; the current induces a magnetic field in this material.

Electromagnetic induction: The phenomenon in which a changing electromagnetic field induces a current to flow through a nearby conductor.

Electromagnetic radiation: Energy in the form of electromagnetic waves, or photons, that travel at the speed of light; such waves generate both electric and magnetic fields as they propagate. The energy of an electromagnetic wave varies inversely with its wavelength. **Gamma rays** have the highest energy and shortest wavelength, followed in order of descending energy and increasing wavelength by **x-rays, ultraviolet radiation, visible light, infrared radiation,** and **radio waves.**

Electromotive force (voltage): The force exerted in accelerating electrons along a circuit to form a current.

Electrons: One of the three components—with protons and neutrons—of atoms. Electrons have a negative electric charge and orbit the atom's nucleus.

Energy level: Any orbit in which the electrons surrounding an atomic nucleus may reside.

Evaporation: The process by which a liquid slowly vaporizes.

Ferromagnetic material: Any material, such as iron, that can be magnetized.

Filament: The thin thread in incandescent lights that glows when heated by electric current.

Fluorescent light: Light generated when an electric current excites gaseous mercury atoms; these atoms then emit ultraviolet radiation that causes a chemical called a phosphor to glow.

Focal length: The distance from the focal point to the center of a lens or mirror.

Focal point: The spot at which all light waves meet as they either reflect off a mirror or pass through a lens.

Fossil fuel: Any substance, such as oil, coal, or natural gas, generated by the decay of organic matter millions of years ago.

Frequency: The number of wave crests in a moving wave that pass a given point per second.

Friction: A force that prevents motion between objects.

Fundamental tone: The sound produced by the longest possible wavelength of a standing wave; in musical instruments, the fundamental tone is the lowest-frequency sound generated.

Gear ratio: The ratio of gear sizes or number of teeth for two gears either in contact with one another or connected by a chain.

Geiger counter: A device that measures radioactivity by counting the number of charged decay products that strike it.

Generator: Any machine that converts mechanical motion into electric current.

Geothermal power: The use of steam produced naturally in deep underground wells to run a turbine and generate electricity.

Gravitational field: The space through which a body's gravitational force can be felt.

Gravity: The force responsible for the mutual attraction of separate masses. The gravitational force between two objects is proportional to their mass and the distance between them.

Ground state: The lowest energy level of an electron.

Heat of transformation: The energy necessary to induce a phase change in a substance.

Incandescent light: Light generated by the electrical heating of a thin filament; as the filament heats up, it gives off light.

Inertia: The tendency of a moving body to remain moving and of a stationary body to remain motionless.

Insulator: A poor conductor of heat or electricity.

Interference: The property of light by which light waves strengthen or cancel each other when they meet.

Kinetic energy: A measure of an object's energy of motion; the faster an object moves, the greater is its kinetic energy.

Laser: A device that produces a very strong beam of light that has only one wavelength.

Light: Electromagnetic radiation with wavelengths between about .000015 inch and .00003 inch; such wavelengths are perceived by the human eye as colors.

Magnetic field: The area throughout which the attractive or repellent force of a magnet can be felt.

Magnetic pole: The ends of a magnet, called north and south, where a magnetic field respectively emanates or converges.

Magnetism: The force of attraction or repulsion between two objects that have molecules arranged in such a way that they generate a magnetic field.

Mass: A measure of the total amount of material in an object, determined by its tendency to resist acceleration.

Mechanical advantage: The degree to which a simple machine changes the effort necessary to do a job.

Neutrino: A subatomic particle that possesses no electric charge and little or no mass.

Neutrons: One of the three constituent parts—with protons and electrons—of an atom; the neutron resides in the atom's nucleus and possesses no electric charge.

Node: A point along a standing wave that has zero amplitude.

N-type silicon: Silicon that has an excess of negative charge.

Nuclear energy: A method of generating electricity in which the heat from radioactive decay is used to boil water; the resulting steam is used to spin a turbine.

Nucleus: The center of an atom around which the electrons orbit; it consists of the atom's protons and neutrons.

Objective lens: The lens on some types of telescopes that forms the image seen by the viewer.

Object wave: A beam of laser light used in making holograms that reflects off the object being photographed onto a piece of film.

Ocean thermal power: A method of generating electricity in which surface water evaporates a liquid with a low boiling point; the resulting vapor is used to spin a turbine.

Ocular lens: A lens that acts as the eyepiece.

Oscilloscope: A machine that turns sound waves into electronic signals and displays the signals on a screen for analysis.

Overtone: The sound produced by a standing wave that has a wavelength equal to a specific fraction of its fundamental tone.

Oxidant: The portion of rocket fuel that provides oxygen, necessary for burning the fuel.

Phosphor: A chemical substance that emits light when excited by radiation.

Positron: A subatomic particle that has the same mass as an electron but possesses a positive charge.

Prism: A device that separates white light into its component colors—red, orange, yellow, green, blue, indigo, and violet.

Propellant: A substance that provides thrust when burned such as the fuel used in rockets.

Protons: One of the three constituents—with neutrons and electrons—of atoms; protons reside in the atom's nucleus and possess a positive charge.

P-type silicon: Silicon that carries a positive electric charge.

Radioactivity: The energy released when an atomic nucleus breaks up.

Real image: The image formed by a lens or mirror where light rays cross.

Reference wave: A beam of light used in making holograms that strikes the same piece of film as the object wave but does not reflect off the object being photographed.

Reflection: The property of light or sound by which it bounces off surfaces.

Refraction: The property of light or sound by which it changes direction when passing from one medium to another.

Scintillation counter: A device that produces an electric signal whenever a charged particle hits it.

Semiconductor: Any material, such as silicon, that can either conduct or block the flow of electricity.

Solar power: The process of generating electricity from the sun. Heat from the sun can be used to turn water into steam to drive a turbine, or sunlight can be used to power a solar cell.

Solenoid: A coil of wire wrapped around a ferromagnetic material to produce an electromagnet.

Sonic boom: A loud noise produced by the rapid expansion of air molecules when an object exceeds the speed of sound.

Sound wave: A mechanical wave formed from the alternating compression and expansion of the substance through which the wave travels.

Static electricity: A buildup on an object of either negative charge, from the gain of electrons, or positive charge, from the loss of electrons.

Superconductivity: A phenomenon in which some materials, when cooled to an extremely low temperature, conduct electricity without resistance.

Sympathetic vibration: A phenomenon in which the sound waves generated by a vibrating object, such as a tuning fork, induce a nearby identical object to vibrate.

Temperature: An indirect measurement of the average speed of vibration of the molecules of a substance.

Thermal conductivity: A measure of how well or poorly a material permits the passage of heat.

Thermal energy: The amount of internal energy contained by a substance; it is the sum of the kinetic energies of all the molecules in the substance, determined by the substance's temperature.

Thermoelectric power: A method of generating electricity in which the heat from the burning of fossil fuels turns water into steam; the steam then turns the blades of a turbine.

Timbre: The distinctive sound produced by a particular musical instrument; it is the product of the instrument's range of tones and the materials used in its construction.

Torque: Any force that acts to turn an object.

Transistor: A semiconductor that can be used as a switch in electronic circuits.

Transition point: The temperature at which a conductor of electricity loses all resistance and becomes a superconductor.

Transverse wave: A wave in which the motion of the medium is perpendicular to the motion of the wave front.

Vaporization: The process in which a solid or liquid changes phase into a gas.

Vapor pressure: The pressure exerted near the surface of a liquid by evaporated molecules of the liquid.

Vector: Any quantity that indicates magnitude and direction.

Virtual image: An image formed by a lens or a mirror that makes rays of light spread out from a common apparent source.

Viscosity: The tendency of a liquid to resist flowing because of friction between the liquid's molecules.

Voltage: The force exerted in accelerating electrons along a circuit to form a current.

Voltage drop: The decrease in the voltage of a circuit that occurs when current passes through a resistor.

Voltmeter: A device that measures electrical voltage.

Volume: The amount of space taken up by a substance.

Wave front: The moving crest of a wave.

Wavelength: The distance between the crests of a wave.

Index

79; vs. superconductors, *93*
Field lines. *See* Magnetic field lines
Filament of incandescent bulb, *72-73*
First-class levers, *43*
First law of motion, Newton's, 24, 28
Fission, nuclear, power production by, *108-109;* reactor core, *94-95, 108*
Fizeau, Armand, experiment by, *118-119*
Flagpole, fixed pulley atop, *48*
Floating, *8-9*
Fluids. *See* Gases; Liquids
Fluorescent lamps, 72, *73*
Focal point: through lenses, *116, 122;* reflection from curved surface, *114-115*
Forces, kinds of, 4; buoyancy vs. gravity, *4-5, 8-9, 10-11;* lift and drag in hang gliding, *14, 15;* Magnus effect, *34, 35;* on roller coaster, *30-31;* on sailboat, *12-13;* on skier, *26-27;* on surfboard, 38; torque, *32;* on train passengers, *28-29. See also* Electricity; Friction; Gravity; Machines, simple; Magnetism; Pressure
Fossil fuels, energy from, and thermoelectric power, *100-101*
Foucault, Jean, experiment by, 118, *119*
Free electrons: in conductors, *82, 84;* radioactive decay and, *90;* in semiconductors, *84*
Freewheel gear, bicycle's, *46-47*
Freezing of water, *66-67*
Frequency of sound, 128, 131, *135;* and Doppler effect, 138; of tuning forks, 142
Friction: and skiers, *26-27;* and static electricity, 70, *71;* and water flow, *20, 21*
Fulcrum, lever's, *42, 43*
Fundamental tone, *134, 137*

G

Galileo Galilei, 28; experiment by, *29*
Galvanometers, *76, 96*
Gamma decay, *91*
Gases: in fluorescent lamps, 72, *73;* lighter-than-air, 10; pressure, temperature, and volume of, *11. See also* Air; Water vapor
Gear ratios, bicycle's, 46, *charts* 46
Gears on bicycle, *46-47*
Geiger counters, *91;* working of, *90, 91*
Generators, electric. *See* Electricity, generating
Geostationary satellites, 37

Geothermal power generation, *102-103*
Geysers, 102
Gliders, hang, *14-15*
Goose, feathers of, *60*
Gravity, 4, 6; vs. buoyancy, in air, *4-5, 10-11;* vs. buoyancy, in water, *8-9;* center of, ship's, *9;* center of, top's, *32, 33;* escape of, by three-stage rocket, *18-19;* and inclined plane, *44;* vs. inertia, *28, 29, 30, 31, 37;* lift vs., in hang gliding, *14, 15;* and skiers, *26-27;* viscosity vs., and whirlpool formation, *20;* and weight, *6-7*
Gravity wells, *7*
Gyroscope, 32

H

Hang gliders, *14-15*
Heat: conductivity, *chart* 61; extreme, measuring, *56-57;* geothermal energy, *102-103;* loss of, insulation against, *60-61;* in nuclear reactor, *109;* and phase changes, *22-23, 52-53, 54-55, 62-63;* in sauna, effects of, *64-65;* solar, as power source, 110, *111;* spreading of, in fluids, *58-59;* in thermoelectric plant, *100-101;* water vapor's transfer of, *64*
Heat energy vs. thermal energy, 52
Heating: of air, *10-11;* convection by, *58-59;* in steamer, *65*
Helical springs, *51*
Hoists, *49*
Holes in semiconductors, *84, 85*
Holograms, *124-125*
Hooke, Robert: Hooke's law, 50
Hot-air balloons, *4-5, 10-11*
Hull tanks for ships, use of, *9*
Humidity in sauna, effect of, *64-65*
Hydroelectric power plant, *98-99*
Hydrogen and oxygen: liquid, as rocket fuel, 18; in water molecules, *54-55*

I

Ice: formation of, *66-67;* phase change in, heat and, *52-53, 54-55;* skating on, 26, *27*
Impulse turbine, *99*
Incandescent bulb, working of, *72-73*
Inclined planes, *44-45*
Induction, electromagnetic, 94
Inertia, *28-29;* Galileo's experiment, *29;* vs. gravity, *28, 29, 30, 31, 37;* law of, 24, 28; and train passengers, *28-29*
Infrared radiation, measuring, *56-57*

Instruments. *See* Musical instruments
Insulation: electrical, *82, 83, 84;* thermal, *60-61*
Intercom, working of, *84, 85*
Interference of light waves, 112, *120-121;* and holograms, *124, 125*
Iron: molten, measuring temperature of, *56-57. See also* Ferromagnetic materials

J

Jackets, down, insulation by, *60-61*
Jackscrew, *45*
Japan: Atomic Energy Research Institute, nuclear power plant at, *109;* superconducting train design, *93*
Jet planes, sonic booms from, *140-141*

K

Kamerlingh Onnes, Heike, 92
Kinetic energy: of molecules, 23, 52; of rolled ball, *29;* of roller coaster, *31*

L

Lamps, electricity illuminating, *72-73*
Lasers, *112-113, 122-123;* and holograms, *124, 125;* speed of light measured with, 119
Latent heat of fusion, defined, 54
Laws of motion, Newton's, 18, 24, 28
Leaf springs, *51*
Lenses, *116-117;* natural light vs. lasers through, *122*
Lever action and screws, *44-45*
Levers, *42-43*
Lift and drag in hang gliding, *14, 15*
Light, 112-127; corpuscular vs. wave theory of, 112; curved surfaces, reflection from, *114-115;* electricity and, *72-73;* and holograms, *124-125;* lasers, *112-113, 119, 122-123, 124, 125;* through lenses, *116-117, 122;* properties of, 112; and soap bubbles, *120-121;* spectrum of, *120;* speed of, measuring, *118-119;* speed of nearing, *126-127;* in temperature measurement, 56, *57*
Light bulbs, working of, *72-73*
Liquids: contraction of, 66; freezing of, *66-67;* rocket fuel, *18. See also* Water
Lithium 8, beta decay of, *91*

M

Machines, simple, 40-51; inclined planes, *44-45;* levers, *42-43;* pulleys, *48-49;* screws, *44-45;* springs, *50-51;* wheel and axle, bicycle's use of, *46-47*

Staff for
UNDERSTANDING SCIENCE & NATURE

Editorial Directors: Patricia Daniels, Allan Fallow, Karin Kinney
Writer: Mark Galan
Assistant Editor/Research: Elizabeth Thompson
Editorial Assistant: Louisa Potter
Production Manager: Prudence G. Harris
Senior Copy Coordinator: Jill Lai Miller
Production: Celia Beattie
Library: Louise D. Forstall
Computer Composition: Deborah G. Tait (Manager), Monika D. Thayer, Janet Barnes Syring, Lillian Daniels

Special Contributors, Text: Joe Alper, Margery duMond, Barbara C. Mallen, Gina Maranto, Mark Washburn
Research: Patricia N. Holland
Design/Illustration: Antonio Alcalá, Caroline Brock, Nicholas Fasciano, Catherine D. Mason, Stephen Wagner
Photography: Fil Hunter; David Parker, Science Photo Library/Photo Researchers, Inc.; Chuck O'Rear, Bill Ross, West Light
Index: Barbara L. Klein
Acknowledgments: Amtrak; Brahm Opticians of Old Town, Alexandria, Virginia; KENETECH/U.S. Windpower, Inc.; Transrapid International

Consultant:
Andrew Pogan is a high-school teacher of chemistry and physics in Montgomery County, Maryland.

Library of Congress Cataloging-in-Publication Data
Physical forces/ editors of Time-Life Books
       p.   cm. — (Understanding science & nature)
    Summary: Questions and answers introduce such physical phenomena as force, motion, magnetism, heat, and sound.
    ISBN 0-8094-9675-5 (trade) — ISBN 0-8094-9676-3 (lib.)
    1. Physics—Miscellanea—Juvenile literature.
    [1. Physics—Miscellanea.   2. Questions and answers.]
    I. Time-Life Books.   II. Series.
    QC25.P48   1992
    530—dc20   92-6937
                                          CIP
                                        AC

TIME-LIFE for CHILDREN ™

Publisher: Robert H. Smith
Associate Publisher and Managing Editor: Neil Kagan
Assistant Managing Editor: Patricia Daniels
Editorial Directors: Jean Burke Crawford, Allan Fallow, Karin Kinney, Sara Mark, Elizabeth Ward
Director of Marketing: Margaret Mooney
Product Managers: Cassandra Ford, Shelley L. Schimkus
Director of Finance: Lisa Peterson
Financial Analyst: Patricia Vanderslice
Administrative Assistant: Barbara A. Jones
Special Contributor: Jacqueline A. Ball

Original English translation by International Editorial Services Inc./ C. E. Berry

Second printing 1993. Printed in U.S.A.
Published simultaneously in Canada.
Time Life Inc. is a wholly owned subsidiary of
THE TIME INC. BOOK COMPANY.
TIME-LIFE is a trademark of Time Warner Inc. U.S.A.
For subscription information, call 1-800-621-7026.

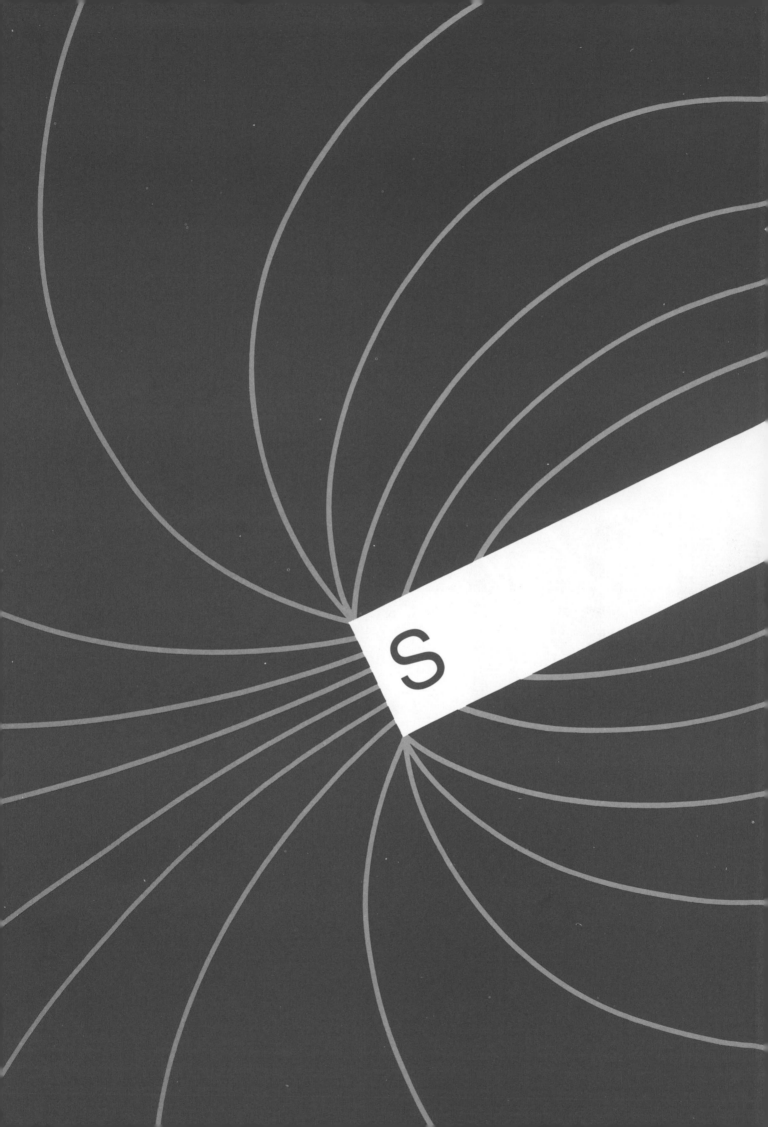